CW00550752

# God's

# Secret

# Weapon

By
Merlin
Carothers

Our special thanks to Hope Welch for contributing her editing
skills in the writing of this book.


Unless otherwise identified, all scripture references are taken
from The Living Bible, translated by Ken Taylor, Tyndale House,
Wheaton, Illinois, 1971.

# Books by Merlin Carothers

# Table of Contents

## Chapter 1
## *Increasing Every Day*

Jesus taught His disciples how to walk on water, heal all manner of diseases, and find money when they needed it. What a way to live! As marvelous as those capabilities would be, you and I may never achieve them. But we *can* learn how to be filled with the joy Jesus came to give us. **It is possible!** But how? This book contains simple answers for anyone who longs for a happier life.

We all want experiences that overwhelm us with joy. However, another experience is far more desirable. It is learning how to have *increasing* joy.

God occasionally gives us experiences that suddenly overwhelm us with happiness. But He wants our lives to follow the "always increasing" pattern of Jesus' life (see Luke 2:52).

We cannot experience joy without peace. God wants to give us His peace, although it may seem confusing at first. After all, it's described as:

*The peace of God, which transcends all under-standing* . . . . (Phil. 4:7 NIV)

We can only begin to understand this peace as it

takes root and grows in us. The more it grows, the more we want it to grow. In fact, Paul writes:

*Let the peace of Christ rule in your hearts . . . .* (Col. 3:15 NIV)

Without God's peace we are unable to feel confident that He is in charge of the earth and everything on it. Ah, peace of heart and mind! Without it, nothing else is valuable. Peace brings joy.

Men and women can be at the very top of successful careers with huge financial resources, good health and great looks, yet be absolutely miserable. Or, they may have moderate success, fair health, average appearance, and still be miserable. Either way, they lack the one ingredient that humans need: peace of heart and mind. This treasure of peace is for all Christians.

When we believe in and trust Jesus as our Savior, we become God's children. *God's children!* What an event to celebrate! Talk about having a reason to rejoice! At that moment, we might want to leave this earth with all its problems. However, God's plan calls for us to remain here while we learn how to grow in favor with Him like Jesus did.

Jesus taught His disciples how they could have a joy that God designed to fit every person on earth:

*Peace I leave with you; my peace I give you . . . . Do not let your hearts be troubled and do not be afraid.* (John 14:27 NIV)

Think of it: He wants us to learn how to *never* be troubled or afraid. This is Good News! He gave us such clear instructions:

*Do not.* One with authority spoke these words. We may ignore His authority, but we cannot escape the results of doing so.

*Do not let.* This means we have the *power* to *not do* something. However, God does not take from us the consequence of being troubled if that is what we choose.

*Do not be troubled.* Jesus knows all about our problems and how they affect us. He explains God's will for us in every situation: d*o not be troubled*. As we practice obeying, we are changed – just as Jesus knew we would be. We learn the joy of having the peace He had, and *why* He told us not to be troubled.

In John's gospel, chapter ten, Jesus compares Himself to a shepherd who loves his sheep; He wants us to believe that He will use all His authority and power to care for us. But, like sheep, we are often afraid.

Phillip Keller was a shepherd for many years. In his book, *A Shepherd Looks At Psalm 23,* he explains that sheep will not lie down if they sense *anything* that might be dangerous. Even the sudden appearance of a rabbit can cause an entire flock of sheep to panic.

Like sheep, we are often convinced that we have something to be troubled about. Our fallen nature tempts us to be anxious about many things. We quickly disregard Jesus' promise to always take care of us. We forget what He said about not letting our hearts be troubled.

Most of us have been troubled at least a million times. We have learned and practiced the habit of being troubled. So we have to *relearn* how to think and react. There is no "instant" way, that I know of, to be free from ever feeling troubled. But as we learn to obey Jesus' command, we will experience more of Heaven's joy.

Even after I had read and memorized Jesus' promise to lead us into peace and joy that are exceedingly and abundantly greater than we could even hope for, I was troubled about many things. Then I learned how to experience His joy! Once our hearts taste the incredible greatness of what God wants to give us, we are willing to spend our lives learning how to receive from Him. I want to give you one of the rich treasures that He gave me. It may be the most valuable gift that anyone has ever given you.

Perhaps you are troubled about family, work, finances, health, traffic, politics or world conditions. It would do no good for me to say, "Cheer up and be happy." So I'll explain what happened to me, and hope that you will understand what it means.

A voice within me said, "Merlin, listen."

It was so clear that it captured all my attention.

"Merlin, do not be troubled about anything."

I heard the words, but did not understand what they *meant*.

"Listen to the words of Jesus!"

I remembered that He told His disciples:

*I am with you always(s), even to the end of the world.* (Mt. 28:20)

I tried listening more intently.

"Merlin, do not be troubled about anything."

The words were repeated several times.

The longer I listened, the quieter my spirit became. It grew increasingly clear to me that God did not want me to be troubled – about anything. Then I spoke:

"Thank You, God, for helping me." I said this over and over as if speaking directly to Him. I heard:

"You are listening."

It was as if God had lifted me into another world and held me there while He exposed my soul to what it was like to . . . as best I can describe it, to believe Him. The experience was so incredible that it changed me for the rest of my life.

Now, whenever I'm tempted to be troubled about something, I center my attention on the message He gave me and the words Jesus spoke to His disciples. When I do this, my mind is over-whelmed by His peace, rather than by the troubles that circumstances seem to create. I recommend that you do the same. This understanding has changed my attitude and the way I respond to things that once made me feel stressed.

Jesus had no home of His own, no possessions, no position, no formal schooling and no money, but He had power. His words caused demons to flee, sickness to vanish, and the dead to live.

Try to imagine the peace of heart and mind Jesus had. He wanted us to enjoy that same peace, as His gift to us. I have learned to enjoy more of that peace, and that is why I'm writing this book. My hope is that you will:

*Fan into flame the gift of God, which is in you . . . .* (2 Tim. 1:6 NIV)

Think of it! His gift of joy is in you, like a fire that can keep burning brighter and brighter!

*God's Secret Weapon*

# Chapter 2
## *What We Want*

Adam and Eve did not believe that God was working for their good; they did what *they* wanted to do. We know the results. What *we* want to do often leads to results that *we* do not want.

We often want, and indulge in, things that are not good for us. What happens then? Sooner or later the not-so-pleasing result is that we are forced to "face the music."

We may ask ourselves, "Why do I feel so unhappy?" We feel as if our lives just aren't going the way they should be. But our wanting things to change does not mean they *should* change!

Our sin nature cries out for, even demands, pleasure. It wants gratification, no matter the cost. It can drive us to satisfy passions that are self-destructive.

I had been taught to believe that stealing was wrong, but my mind searched for exceptions to that rule. Exceptions! That's what we often seek.

Back in my teens I wanted to travel. Therefore, I *needed* wheels. I convinced myself that it was okay to "borrow" another person's car. There was no need to keep the car for more than a couple of weeks, so it wasn't *really* stealing. I had never had a car, and would soon be going overseas to war. The owner's insurance would reimburse him for the loss, and anyhow, *he* didn't have to go into combat where he might lose *his* life. Does my reasoning sound familiar?

On my way I went, and for a time it was exciting. Wheels! Travel! Fun! Then guilt set in. The police might catch me! My initial pleasure began to fade.

My parents taught me that it was not good to drink alcohol. But, once again, I *needed* to have fun! It seemed that all I had ever done was work and obey other people's rules. Now it was time for me to do what *I* wanted to do!

It sounded reasonable at the time. So, my sin nature led me to places where I could enjoy the gratification of getting intoxicated. It was fun, but payback time always followed.

Some folks are lured to drugs. It seems right. They like it. Soon they need them again. The logic goes, "I want it; therefore I must have it." Eventually that "pleasure" demands its toll in health and happiness.

We're very good at convincing ourselves that we should do what we think we will enjoy. Because of our fallen nature, we, like Adam and Eve, may make decisions that bring suffering rather than joy. If you have already fallen into this ambush, you understand. We are all subject to repeating past mistakes, over and over again. But there is a way out: we can discover ever-increasing joy and happiness!

Jesus urges us to learn God's secret of *increasing joy*, rather than falling into the trap of ever-*decreasing* pleasure.

We tend to focus on the pleasures of immorality, rather than its potential for suffering. We rationalize, "God gave me the desire, so He will understand if I do what seems okay to me." Satan tells us that we are in charge, while in reality, we are giving over control to his destructive power.

The master we choose will gradually manipulate our thoughts:

> *Don't you know that when you offer yourselves to someone to obey . . . you are slaves to the one whom you obey . . . ?* (Rom. 6:16 NIV)

When I saw the atrocities committed by German soldiers as an Airborne Infantryman during WWII, I began to despise all Germans. Their SS Troops were especially horrendous. The very word *German* made me angry.

When the war was over, I still expected that every German citizen was plotting something evil. Later, I realized that the German people are the same as we are – some good and others not. After getting acquainted with the people, I understood what had happened to them.

Adolph Hitler had promised a depressed, hungry people that he would give them jobs, food and prosperity. And he did.

Step by step, Hitler gradually took over everything – even the way German people thought – to the point where many became his pawns. Eventually he had so much power that the average person could do nothing but obey or be executed. Their obedience to Hitler nearly caused the destruction of the entire nation. City after city was reduced to rubble, with not one building left standing.

Satan promises us pleasure and satisfaction. He craftily keeps some of his promises. Then he gradually takes control of our minds, and we lose nearly everything that could bring us happiness.

Many people are unaware of how seductive evil can be.

God designed us for happiness, and He has provided a way for us to have ever-*increasing* happiness! He also warns of the demonic force that opposes the Holy Spirit:

*These two forces within us are constantly fighting each other to win control over us, and our wishes are never free from their pressures.* (Gal. 5:17)

Suppose you build and sell a product; once it is sold, you have no control over how it is used. However, you *could* design your product in such a way that it needs something only *you* can supply. That way, the owner would need to come back to you. This is the way God designed us!

*We need the happiness that only God can supply!*

We try many substitutes: pleasures, power, and success. But they all break down. They will never be able to fulfill what God has designed us to need: His own solution for a happy life.

Children are born crying, and they practice that fine art for the first few months of their lives. Then they learn the far more enjoyable art of laughing. Their new behavior makes everyone happier, including family, friends and bystanders. But with age, that carefree laugher becomes more and more infrequent.

Jesus came to restore and amplify everyone's ability to laugh. He came to bring us joy. He encouraged us to become more like "little children."

It brings me joy to remember that:

*I can do everything God asks me to with the help of Christ who gives me the strength and power.* (Phil. 4:13)

One day, as I was considering this verse, my

thoughts were interrupted by the question, *What things can you do through Christ?* I had never tried to list exactly what I could do through Christ. So I began a list. I can:

1. Always be full of joy in the Lord (Phil. 4:4).

*2.* Shout unto God with the voice of triumph (Ps. 47:1 KJV).

3. Have a new song in my mouth; many shall see it, and shall trust in the LORD (Ps. 40:3 KJV).

4. Be filled with all joy and peace in believing through the power of the Holy Spirit (Rom. 15:13 KJV).

5. Be strong in the Lord, and in the power of His might (Eph. 6:10 KJV).

6. Have nothing, and yet possess everything (2 Cor. 6:10 NIV).

7. Have the full measure of Christ's joy (John 17:13 NIV).

These are all things that God wants us to do. They're also things that I want to do! Who wouldn't want to have the full measure of Christ's joy? What unlimited potential God has given us! Too often we are controlled by circumstances instead of using the authority Christ has given us.

If you were to inherit a large fortune you might be quick to rejoice, thank God, and maybe even smile a lot. But Jesus gives us something much greater than material wealth: He gives us victory!

*Thanks be to God! He gives us the victory through our Lord Jesus Christ.* (1 Cor. 15:57 NIV)

Now *that* is a reason to smile!

## Chapter 3
## *"Running Over" Blessings*

*Don't just think about your own affairs, but be interested in others too, and in what they are doing.* (Phil. 2:4)

We easily become so focused on our own affairs that we do not think about the concerns of others. But we can change our way of thinking, and God gives us incentives to do so:

*Give, and it will be given to you. A good measure, pressed down, shaken together and running over, will be poured into your lap. For with the measure you use, it will be measured to you.* (Luke 6:38 NIV)

Jesus didn't promise that if we bless another person, that person would respond favorably to us. He did promise that God will give us a *good measure* of *pressed down and running over* blessings!

So if we want to be happier, more joyful people, we can bring happiness to others and God will give us "running over" blessings. What an offer! You may ask, does this *really* work? We can find out for ourselves!

17

God already knows that we tend to center our attention on ourselves. Our past experiences may cause us to hesitate in acting toward certain types of people as we know we should. Since God understands, He tells us:

*As we have opportunity, let us do good to all people. . . .* (Gal. 6:10 NIV)

We don't need to ponder how deserving people may be. God says just go ahead and do good at every opportunity, and *I will* bless you.

Since Jesus taught us to love others, it may be quite easy for us to say, "Of course I love everyone. I'm a Christian." But what did Jesus mean when He used the word *love?* He said:

*Love each other just as much as I love you.* (John 13:34)

Jesus also said:

*Do for others what you want them to do for you.* (Mt. 7:12)

There is often a big difference between what we *have been doing* and what we *should be doing.* We do not think of others as we would like them to think about us. For example, we want other people to like us and to overlook our faults and failures. When we dislike someone, we have "valid" reasons. But, for sure, we would like others to disregard their "valid" reasons for disliking us! We may not be perfect, but we can look for ways to both love and like people more than we do.

When we demonstrate Christ's love for people, we cause them to see Him! He wants us to demonstrate His love – to everyone – whenever we have an opportunity to do so. We can look for opportunities!

God loves us because of *who He is.*

We can learn to love others because of who *we* are, and not because of who *they are.*

With each new day, God reveals more of the changes that need to be made in me. As He does this, He clearly demonstrates that He is keeping His promise to give me His *running over* joy! Here is one example of how He is teaching me.

My wife Mary and I were enjoying a dish of ice cream in an ice cream shop when a small child began hollering and shattered the quiet atmosphere. The mother was smiling at the child and this seemed to encourage the child to holler more. I began thinking of how rude it was for this mother to force all the other customers to listen to her misbehaving child. She should take the child outside

– anywhere but here in *my* space.

After we left the shop, the Holy Spirit began to ask me if I had done anything to help the mother. *Did I pray for her?* Well, no. *Why not? Did I look for a way to be a blessing to her?* No. *Why not?* I was thinking of ways she should be blessing me. I was not thinking:

*Your attitude should be the same as that of Christ Jesus . . . .* (Phil. 2:5 NIV)

Later the Holy Spirit asked me, "What if: the mother had saved money for weeks just so she could take her child for this special treat; or the child had just recovered from a serious illness; or the mother had just died and this lady was doing her best to care for the child?" More questions came and I began to weep. Whatever the conditions were, I had judged this woman instead of loving her as Jesus would have. I have so many things to learn!

Here is an important question: what do you want people to be thinking when they look at you? We can learn to think about others the way that we would like them to think about us. Yes, that may be difficult for us to do, but loving others *as much as Jesus loves us* isn't easy either!

We look at another person and think thoughts

such as: "What a selfish, rude person they are." You may ask, "But if a person is selfish and rude, what else *could* I be thinking when I look at them?"

That is the question, isn't it? What *should* we think? We all need to decide what we *should* think about others and how our thoughts will affect both them and us.

Think about the type of person the Apostle Paul was before his conversion. He was considerably more than just selfish or rude: he went from town to town looking for people called "Christians" so he could have them executed! He was a really bad person. I would not have liked him. Neither would I have seen the tremendous potential that God saw in him. How many people do we meet that have great potential we don't see?

Jesus spoke to Paul and he became a tool in God's hands. God used Paul to lead multitudes of people to believe in and follow Jesus. God also wants to use us, and He will, as long as we learn to think of and act toward people as Jesus did.

Here is a good place for us to begin:

*Overwhelming victory is ours through Christ who loved us enough to die for us.* (Rom. 8:37)

With Jesus' *overwhelming victory* working in us, difficult things become possible! We can change our thoughts and even the way we feel about people.

We receive joy when we believe that people like us. Would it be possible for us to find new ways to like the "unlikable" so that they, too, might receive joy?

Should we believe that people like us because we are such good people? No. We can believe that because Jesus is in us and has made each of us a new person, He is making us likeable! Could we also believe that He is changing someone *else* into a likeable person?

It came as a life-giving revelation to me that people will like me when they see Jesus in me. And I can like *them* because of what Jesus is doing *in me*! Jesus gives us a clue to success: think of others as better than yourself (see Phil. 2:3). In many cases that's a real challenge.

I have talked with people who believe that no one likes them. They sometimes say, "I don't care if people like me. I am what I am." But everyone wants to be liked. Even little children keep trying to get other kids to like them. Popularity is a big thing with young people. As we get older we become more sophisticated and are less obvious about our desire to be liked, but we still enjoy having people demonstrate that they want to be around us. We sometimes do nice things, whether we realize it or not, because we are hoping to get others to appreciate us.

We can sense when another person dislikes us. In the same way, other people usually perceive when we don't like them, even if we try to disguise our true feelings. What you feel in your heart is visible in your eyes, the look on your face, and the way you position your body. If you tell a person that you love them, but they believe that you don't even like them, they will look at you as a hypocrite.

You may despise what Satan has done in a person, but you can still love that person. Once we understand this, and begin to practice it, the Holy Spirit releases new joy in us. We become a little more like Jesus, who freely gave His life to help *every person*.

*Dear friends, let us practice loving each other . . . .* (1 John 4:7)

The more I understand *and practice* these principles, the more I sense Christ's love and joy in me.

Chapter 4

## *God Has A Reason*

I was on a flight from Pittsburgh to Dallas, and a handsome young man was concentrating on the young woman sitting beside him.

For two hours he stroked her hair and face, kissed her over and over, and took her picture dozens of times. They talked and clung to one another for the entire trip. It was obvious the young man was totally smitten with the girl beside him. He was enjoying her so much that he was not interested in anything else. I could only see the top of her head because the back of her seat hid her face from my view. I thought to myself, "What a marvelously beautiful girl she must be!"

As I watched this scene, I realized that it was an excellent illustration of how we Christians should be absorbed in the One we love: Jesus. People cannot see *His* face, but they will be interested if they see our total captivation with Him. They will wonder who this person is that has so completely captured our love. We may never have spoken to them, but they see and study *us*. They may know little or nothing about Jesus, but when they see our joy they want it. They may even ask why we are so happy. What an opportunity to tell them!

God has a reason for putting His joy in us. He wants to use us to draw others to His Son. God knows that everyone wants to be happy. Some people wonder if they will ever find happiness. They have been so disappointed with life that they are not easily convinced by God's promises.

We may wish that we had a special talent that would draw people to Christ – perhaps an athletic ability that everyone admired. But we do not need to have extraordinary talents in order to encourage others to become Christians. We need only to love God. To do that, we must focus our attention on Him. That's what His disciples did. People couldn't help but see the effect Jesus had on His followers:

*They were amazed and realized what being with Jesus had done for them!* (Acts 4:13)

What changes did people see in those who had recently been with Jesus? I believe He had given them joy. How did that happen? They believed what He taught them! Jesus healed people when they believed Him, and He gave joy to those who believed Him. As we learn to believe more of what Jesus teaches, He gives us new joy.

Sometimes I feel overwhelmed with joy. Within me there is a light that seems to surround and lift my heart. My family, neighbors and friends tell me I always seem to be happy. Some say, "You look as if you don't have a care in the world." I ask myself why I should look and feel so happy when many good people have so much gloom.

It's not that I "don't have a care in the world." There are things that I struggle with every hour of every day.

For example, I've had a headache for most of my life, caused by a parachute landing fall in which I was knocked unconscious. It started in 1953 and has steadily worsened over time. Medical tests have predicted dire consequences. The pain has stretched my faith at times, but my inner happiness has continued to increase!

When specialists said I had a heart problem, they scheduled a battery of tests to determine what operation I needed. They were concerned that ten years earlier I had been hospitalized for two weeks with similar symptoms. I've seldom mentioned what happened next because people might perceive my experience as imaginary. Nevertheless, the memory gives me such joy that I have to share it with you.

While I was sitting alone in a doctor's treatment room waiting for the test results, gloom began to surround my heart. It seemed as if an evil force was trying to drag me downward.

Sitting with my eyes closed, head in my hands,

I began to thank God that He was in charge of my life. As I continued thanking Him, joy began to make me want to sing. Then I sensed someone standing on my right, and someone on my left. Their presence was so real that I *knew* they were there. Instantly, the gloom in my heart lifted, and I was completely free of any concern over what the doctor might have to say.

Shortly thereafter, a nurse came and escorted me to the doctor's office. The doctor smiled and told me that I was indeed fortunate. The new tests showed that the previous problem no longer existed.

When I try to explain to others the joy that God has given me, I cannot find adequate words to describe it. But I believe God wants us to have *ever-increasing* joy. That is His plan for each and every one of His children.

My sufferings have been minor compared to what some Christians have endured. And some of them report inner joy that is greater than I have experienced.

James Guthrie was born in Scotland in 1612. He attended St. Andrews University and then became a Presbyterian minister. Because of his faith he was sentenced to be hanged, his head to be stuck on a spike, and his entire estate confiscated. While he was in prison he told his wife that he considered himself fortunate to be hanged on a tree as his Savior was. Before he was hanged in 1661 he said to the crowd that came to watch:

"Blessed be God who has shown mercy to me such a wretch, and has revealed His Son in me . . . . Jesus Christ is my Life and my Light, my Righteousness, my Strength, and my Salvation and all my Desire. Him! O Him, I do with all the strength of my soul commend to you. Bless Him, O my soul, from henceforth even forever. Lord, now lettest Thou thy servant depart in peace for mine eyes have seen Thy salvation."

James Guthrie had found a joy that overwhelmed both his natural concern for his family and the natural fear of his coming execution. You and I may face greater or lesser tragedies, but God can give us joy to fit our exact situation.

Think of the potential that God has to create peace and joy in us!

Jesus told us we could receive *anything* from God if we believed Him (see Mt. 21:22). You may at this moment have little or no joy. In less than a moment, God could flood your heart with joy! What does it take for us to receive such an extraordinary gift from God? Faith. *Believing Him.*

But know this! We cannot believe that we are

unhappy and at the same time believe that we are being filled with joy. The two do not go together.

I have chosen to believe that I am being filled with joy, overflowing with joy, and always learning how to receive more of God's joy. That is what God wants for us! Why should you or I want otherwise? I may not be the happiest man in the world, but I do not know a happier one.

Why do I have this gift of joy? It is God's desire to give His gifts to *anyone who believes Him.*

Do you understand this emphasis on joy? The angel announced the coming of Jesus as good news of **great joy** (see Luke 2:10). This is how God wanted the birth of His Son to be announced; therefore *it is important*!

Some folks react with disapproval when we speak of the importance of Christians having joy. They see people who are not Christians intent on having fun, and feel we should be different. They may point to Scripture and insist that we should be willing to carry heavy loads, but they miss the wonderful blessings of Jesus' promise:

> *Take my yoke upon you and learn from me . . . and you will find rest for your souls.* (Mt. 11:29 NIV)

The purpose of a yoke was to make it *easier* for an ox to pull its load. A good yoke was smooth, designed to prevent painful and disabling sores. Jesus knows how painful our lives can be. He wants to help us. One of the ways He helps us is by giving us joyful hearts.

I believe that Satan does everything he can to prevent Christians from experiencing joy. He strives to convince us that we should feel and act unhappy. But our lack of joy influences others to regard Christianity as an unattractive option.

Think of parents gazing at their small child. What gives them joy? Seeing their child happy! We are God's children, and He is pleased when we have great joy.

What comes to the minds of a couple with no children when they see another couple with a happy child? They long for a child of their own. The same principle applies to our joy. When we radiate joy, we draw others to the source of our joy: Jesus.

*God's Secret Weapon*

## Chapter 5
### *Have A Little Faith*

We were alive, but we couldn't see or even breathe. That's because we hadn't been born yet. Then, after we were born, our process of learning about this world began.

Jesus described our relationship with Him as one of being "born again" (see John 3:3-7). Before that happens, we may think of ourselves as being alive, but we do not have a life that will last *forever*. We can't really see truth; we can't experience the breath of the Holy Spirit. When we're born again, we're brought into real life! That "forever life" changes us, and from that moment on we have new potential to grow and become more pleasing to God. There is such joy in pleasing God!

There are some who choose to believe that there is no God. When they make that decision, does it give them joy? None, that I've heard of. Others decide that they don't know if there is a God. Again, the belief they have chosen gives them no joy. They are without God and without hope (see Eph. 2:12). Make no mistake: both the atheist and the agnostic have *chosen* to believe what they believe:

*But God shows his anger from heaven against all sinful, evil men who push away the truth from them. For the truth about God is known to them instinctively; God has put this knowledge in their hearts. Since earliest times men have seen the earth and sky and all God made, and have known of his existence and great eternal power. So **they will have no excuse** . . .* (Rom.1:18-20, **emphasis mine**)

Self-help advocates teach that we need to believe in ourselves. While it is true that a lack of self-confidence can cause people to fail, self-confidence is definitely *not* all we need.

A baseball player depends on his fingers as he positions them on his bat. If he were to lose one finger he would have to relearn how to hold his bat. He might still be a successful batter if he worked hard and believed that he could. If he were to lose another finger he would have to work much harder and have even more self-confidence. If he lost a hand there is still a slight possibility that he could learn how to bat well with one arm. But what would happen if he lost his eyesight? Self-confidence will no longer help him to be a successful baseball player.

That's just the way life is. Self-confidence can only take us so far. If our hope for happiness is based on our own power and potential, then we are emotionally crippled.

Jesus emphasized that what we believe is important. God has given us the freedom to decide what we believe. If we are uncertain or have questions, we also have the freedom to seek out the truth.

So what, or who, should we believe in? Jesus said:

*Believe in God, believe also in me.* (John 14:1 KJV)

Why?

*Whoever believes in him* [Christ] *shall not perish but have eternal life.* (John 3:16 NIV)

When a man decides to believe and trust in Jesus, new life changes him. His belief gives him confidence; his life now has purpose. He feels the joy of forgiveness and expects to spend eternity in Heaven. He will look and act differently. How do we acquire this new life, this "forever life?"

First, we believe the greatest miracle of all time – that Jesus forgives and saves us – and we pass from death into life. Then, by faith, we keep moving forward and learning more about the joys that God's Son came to give us. **Our potential to**

**grow in Christ is unlimited!** God offers to bring us into a closer relationship with Him.

As believers, our position before God is awe-inspiring: we are His children!

*How great is the love the Father has lavished on us, that we should be called children of God! And that is what we are!* (1 John 3:1 NIV)

Even the angels wondered how sinful men could be made right with God. Then they learned that one of their missions would be to serve those who believe the Good News about Christ:

*The angels are only spirit-messengers sent out to help and care for those who are to receive his salvation.* (Heb.1:14)

Spiritual truths don't always come with visible evidence. When it comes to faith, the rule of thumb is:

*We live by faith, not by sight.* (2 Cor. 5:7 NIV)

What ever-increasing joy might you have if you have ever-increasing faith?

The people of Jesus' day wanted to see tangible evidence that He was the Son of God. They wanted

Him to do more miracles; but He refused to satisfy them. Within our fallen nature there exists a desire for God to prove himself to us. But faith does not require proof:

*Faith is being sure of what we hope for and certain of what we do not see.* (Heb. 11:1 NIV)

Every day, for thousands of years, men watched what appeared to be the sun going around the earth. They made the natural assumption that what they saw was actually happening. How could they believe otherwise?

Look at the ground and try to imagine that the earth is racing through space, circling the sun, and rotating once every twenty-four hours. Such thoughts would be impossible to fathom if we did not know that the earth is in fact doing this – whether we see and feel it or not.

There was a time when I believed only what I could see and feel. Sometimes what I saw and felt made me happy, but when things changed I became unhappy. That's the destiny of everything that is part of this world: sooner or later it turns into sadness. But everlasting joy is *our* destiny when we have faith that God is *always* working for our good (see Rom. 8:28).

God tells us to have faith in Him, even in the

hard times. He tells us that He is always, in every situation, working for our good. He tells us to trust Him and not to doubt.

In both the Old and New Testaments God rewarded those who believed Him. It is more difficult to have faith in some situations than in others, but the more difficult our situation is, the more important it is that we learn to have faith!

Remember Peter, who by faith stepped out of the boat and walked on water? He began to sink because he shifted his attention from Jesus to what he perceived was a huge problem. You know he was troubled: as a fisherman, everything in his experience told him he was in trouble. Like you and I often do, he paid more attention to his circumstances (the wind and the waves) than he did to Jesus, who has the power to control all things. You and I won't go down if we have faith in God.

Faith that God will help us is essential if we are to have the joy He wants for us. If we set our minds on what *we want*, we will be disappointed. God will not bend His will to suit our wants, no matter how right we think we are.

Having a strong faith does not mean we will always get the things we want or believe we need. **Faith means believing that God is always right, that He loves us perfectly, and that He will always do what is best for us.**

God did not plan for us to always live in protected prosperity. Down through history Christ's followers have been imprisoned, beaten and murdered. Why? Because God had a plan for them – to help people like you and me.

God has a plan for us, too, and His objective is still the same. He wants us to believe in and trust Him, regardless of our circumstances.

Paul's faith helped him deal with the sufferings he endured. Consider his words:

*We have gone hungry and thirsty, without even enough clothes to keep us warm. We have been kicked around without homes of our own. We have worked wearily with our hands to earn our living.* (1 Cor. 4:11-12)

Paul was even put in a prison cell and chained to a stone floor, yet he wrote:

*My God will meet all your needs according to his glorious riches in Christ Jesus.* (Phil. 4:19 NIV)

Now there's a faith that isn't based on circumstances!

Jesus was the perfect example of faith. He was willing to let God work in His life, even through His death on a cross. Jesus said:

*Father, if you are willing, please take away this cup of horror from me. But I want your will, not mine.* (Luke 22:42)

It is especially important for us to understand that when God raised Jesus from the dead, He caused even His crucifixion to work for great good. In the same way, God will work all things for our good. Once we dare to trust Him we will understand that our cross, whatever it may be, can be used by God to accomplish great good:

*[The Lord] turned the intended curse into a blessing for you, because the Lord loves you.* (Deut. 23:5)

God has His plan and only His plan will work for our good. For example, He encourages us to pray for healing. He will heal us – unless He has a better plan. He did not heal Jesus as He hung on the cross. God's plan was for Jesus to bleed, die, and be resurrected so He could bring new life to you and me. He also has a plan for you and me!

We usually want God to skip the hard lessons, but He has the same answer for each of His children. He will do what He, in His loving wisdom, knows is best. The more quickly we learn this the happier we will be. God is not primarily interested in providing us a life without problems. He has a far greater interest.

Because we are His children, God always works for our good. He also wants to work through us to help others. All too often we want Him to bypass the working *through* us and get busy with the working *for* us. We will never be successful in receiving all that He has for us until we learn to trust that He is accomplishing something in us. We need to have faith.

Learning to have faith is a step-by-step process. I enjoy reading and writing, but I probably did not enjoy learning to read or write. My mother taught me to write the alphabet, the days of the week and the months of the year before I began school. Learning has continued over many years and is partly responsible for the pleasure I now have in reading and writing. God wants us to enjoy our step-by-step process of learning to trust Him.

Most of us want to learn how to have more faith. Here is good news: when we thank God, we are *creating faith*! The more we rejoice, the stronger our faith and joy will become.

We are confronted by people and situations that cause us to feel troubled. Rather than thinking about such things, I have learned how incredibly powerful it is to spend time thanking God for the good things that we take for granted: I can see! I can hear, walk, talk, sing, laugh, read, write . . . . God, You forgive me of my mistakes and even my sins!

To be effective, my thanksgiving must come from a place deep within me. By the time I have spent five or ten minutes in this simple act of enjoying God's blessings, I feel an inner joy that is difficult to describe. The troubled thoughts are gone!

One day as I was praying for understanding, Jesus' words filled my mind. I remembered how He explained the coming of the Holy Spirit, shouting to the people:

*Living water shall flow from the inmost being of anyone who believes in me.* (John 7:38)

Believing what Jesus tells us releases a feeling that He described as *living water flowing from our inmost being*! That is what happens as we give thanks to God. I do not want to permit myself to be troubled about anything; it is far better to enjoy His living water. Whenever we are troubled, we can immediately begin to thank God and feel *living water flowing from our inmost being.*

## Chapter 6

## *Ready To Move Mountains?*

Our bodies require food, water and oxygen to be healthy. Do we also need happiness? If you were to ask one thousand doctors if they believe we need happiness to be healthy, every one of them would respond, "Yes." They have seen enough evidence to know that unhappiness causes disease.

When you are unhappy, your body produces a substance that flows from your head to your toes and automatically troubles your health. Why is that? God designed us for happiness! Just as He provides for our needs by supplying us with food, water and oxygen, He has provided a way for us to be happy! And *His* happiness improves our health! How can we experience His happiness? It's going to take some faith.

*If you have faith as small as a mustard seed, you can say to this mountain, "Move from here to there" and it will move. Nothing will be impossible for you.* (Mt.17:20 NIV)

Jesus made this statement 2,000 years ago, and to my knowledge, not one person has moved a physical mountain by their faith. What if you became the first person?

You would make front-page news around the world. The president would probably want you to come to the White House. He might send his plane to pick you up!

World leaders would seek your help once they saw that you could actually move mountains by your faith.

Then, trouble would come. If ten people wanted you to move a mountain, one hundred would say you should leave the mountain alone. Environmentalists would demand a law that made it illegal for anyone to move a mountain without an environmental study.

Terrorists would demand that if you move a mountain, you do it in the name of their god. Some would say that it was Satan who gave you this power to move mountains. What began as a great adventure could quickly become a mountain-sized headache.

I don't think Jesus' point is that we should change the earth's topography. He's giving us an illustration. But an illustration of what? *Nothing will be impossible* for you. Nothing. Not even finding happiness.

Hundreds, thousands, and even millions of people would say if asked, "Yes, God gives me joy and increases my joy when I believe Him." Some report a slight increase in their happiness. Others report a joy that they find difficult to even describe.

Throughout the past two thousand years there have been many reports of people who experienced "great joy" even while they were dying. Often, people who were being executed for their faith in Jesus reported a joy that obliterated even their fear of being tortured. As they were bound to posts and told they would be burned alive, men and women sang hymns of celebration. Even as the flames rose, they sang with joy.

You and I aren't dying. We are living. But we still want to have joy – the kind of joy that helps our ordinary lives to be happy.

Since Jesus said we can move mountains by our faith, we know that – if we believe – we can have **great joy!**

If joy is available to us, why is it that so many people are unhappy? Might the answer be simple? Could it be that we have sought happiness in ways that work *against* God's design for us?

Consider the things that we know do not guarantee us happiness.

Our delight in eating is an example. We enjoy eating, but in a short time the body says, "I want more. I will not be happy unless you give me more." If we follow that leading too often, a doctor will tell us, "Your heart is acting up and you must stop eating some of the things you enjoy."

Eventually we learn that things that give us temporary pleasure can lead to unhappiness. Maybe then we'll be ready to listen to God's remedy: He wants us to find happiness in Him! He designed us so that emotionally, physically and spiritually, we need Him. And there are no limits to the amount of joy He can create in us. **No limits**!

The New Testament uses the word "joy" sixty-three times, often referring to a joy that comes from God. God tells us to rejoice in Him *always* (see Phil 4:4). Is that actually possible?

When I was a young man I observed that many people have happiness stripped from them by others who are uncaring. I decided to get whatever happiness I could, by hook or by crook. I knew that people weren't going to help me, and it seemed obvious that God wasn't going to help me either. Maybe some of us were created to be "the unhappy ones," I thought.

After I became a Christian, I kept telling myself that my faith was weak because I didn't feel happy. I even told God that my faith was weak. My declarations were honest, but the more I thought about my weak faith, the more firmly that fact took root in me.

Finally, I realized that God doesn't want us to dwell on what we lack. Of course, God knows when our faith is weak. But He wants us to dwell on what He can do! I began to confess things that He was doing for me. "God, You are helping me to believe whatever *You* want me to believe. *You are* helping me to believe."

I practice a tune that you older folks may remember, but I use these words:

> I sing because I'm happy,
> And I'm happy because I sing;
> For His eyes are on the praisers,
> And I know He's watching over me.

As I sing these words, joy begins to replace my anxieties. I'm not literally moving mountains, but I have faith that God is working His will in me. God working in us – what an encouraging thought!

*For it is God which worketh in you both to will and to do of his good pleasure.* (Phil. 2:13 KJV)

Surely He who created the universe can work His will in you and me!

*God's Secret Weapon*

Chapter 7
# *The Power of Our Thoughts*

If you cut a finger, you do not need to say to yourself, "Body, get busy and start healing me." The body has been programmed to do what needs to be done. It automatically goes to work on stopping the flow of blood and healing the wound.

When you believe you are in danger, signals go out: the heart starts pumping more blood and everything gets ready to move. Within seconds the body is prepared to escape the danger.

What if we worry about danger when there is no danger? The body still shifts into its danger mode. The heart pounds, breathing changes, and adrenalin flows.

Did you know that the body can receive automatic signals that actually *decrease* health and happiness? If you think, "I'm unhappy," the body shifts into that mode, even if you have no real reason to be unhappy. The Bible offers a positive alternative:

*A cheerful heart has a continual feast.* (Prov. 15:15 TLB)

When the heart is merry, so is the rest of the body. Our bodies react to happiness! Happiness can work in us even when our circumstances aren't ideal, just as the body can be put on high alert when there's nothing to be afraid of. We can choose to be happy.

Try thinking, "I'm happier today than I was yesterday," or, "God is pouring His happiness into my heart." What happens? The more we concentrate on such thoughts, the stronger our joy becomes! Believe it or not, we can have increasing joy – a joy that nothing, and no one, can take away!

Our Designer knows us well. He commands us to do what He knows is best for us. And He wants us to help others learn how they, too, can *rejoice in the Lord always.*

Most of us have learned that bad thoughts make us feel unhappy. We may not have learned that many of these thoughts are avoidable.

"I'm so tired. I'm upset. I'm angry. I can't handle this problem." Such thoughts can affect every organ in our bodies. They are like an invisible virus that makes its way from our heads to our toes.

The Bible warns against such thinking. We can either ignore its wisdom and choose unhappiness, or we can resist our fallen nature and choose thoughts that lift us upward. Instead of thinking, "My life is difficult," we can think, "My life will be easier today because God is working good for me." We can change our thoughts so that they are in agreement with God's Word:

*Whatever is true, whatever is noble, whatever is right, whatever is pure, whatever is lovely, whatever is admirable—if anything is excellent or praiseworthy—think about such things.* (Phil. 4:8 NIV)

That doesn't sound easy, does it? But we are here to learn the lessons that God wants to teach us. Did you know that we could have hundreds of thoughts every day that are *not* excellent, and be completely unaware of it? We need to think about what we're thinking about.

When I was a Private in the Army I walked what seemed like a million miles, and usually thought of nothing other than how much my feet hurt. Now, if I'm not careful, it's easy for me to walk a block and think of nothing but – you guessed it – my feet.

There is a happy chorus that reads:

Joy is the flag flown high
From the castle of my heart

When the King is in residence here.

When I'm tempted to think an unhappy thought, I sometimes think of hoisting a flag of joy while I am displaying a bright smile. This helps to bring my thoughts under the Lord's control.

If we think, "God is blessing me exceedingly and abundantly," every cell of our body will hear that message. Cell by cell, we become joyful people.

If I was confined to a wheelchair and told you with a smile that I was always thinking about how blessed I was to be able to see, hear, and talk, you might respond, "What marvelous, *praiseworthy* thoughts for Merlin to have. I need to learn to think that way too." If *you* have problems, you have the opportunity to influence others to change the way they think about *their* problems.

Remember: your body responds to every thought you have. You have the power to choose what you will think about!

Before we do anything, right or wrong, we first *think* about it. Thoughts are the mechanism by which we get actions into motion. Therefore, consider how crucial it is to decide what you will and will not think about. Your thoughts are your first line of defense against unhappiness.

No matter how confident or successful we are, or how well everything is going for us, we are always at risk: unhappy or undesirable thoughts can take root at any time.

Have you ever done something, and later wished you hadn't? Perhaps you spoke when it would have been better to be silent; or ate something you knew you shouldn't have eaten; or made a purchase you couldn't afford; or watched something that wasn't edifying. The possibilities are unlimited. Now remember that you thought about that action before you engaged in it. You may have debated, "Will I do it or not?" Remember this important fact: We can refuse to even *think* about doing something! It works. Learning that God gives us this authority helps us to avoid a multitude of problems.

Eve lived in a perfect world with no disease and in a garden that had no weeds. Satan invited her to think about a problem that she didn't even have. "Eve, maybe God is withholding something good from you. Maybe if you ate the forbidden fruit something new and good would come to you." Eve listened, *thought*, and then acted. You know the rest.

As king, David had the authority to choose any virgin in his entire kingdom to be his wife. In fact, he had many wives. But when he saw Bathsheba taking a bath on the rooftop of her home, he thought lustful thoughts. He looked, he thought, and he planned. Then he sinned by taking Bathsheba as his own and having her husband killed. And it didn't end there. David's son Solomon followed in his father's footsteps. Solomon took many wives, and they turned his heart to other gods in his old age.

If we want to enjoy *good* things, our first, second and third objectives must be to think *good thoughts*. Think of it: you have the ability and responsibility to choose your thoughts!

Good thoughts produce new life in us. They open up a channel for new happy thoughts. They cause our hearts to respond to God in a brand new way. They lead us into joy. We become receptive to the many good things that Jesus came to give us.

When you *feel* unhappy, stop and realize what is happening in you. What are you thinking? As you carefully guard your mind, you may find that you are thinking something negative.

Successful military leaders have emphasized that, "The most effective defense is to attack." We can mount an attack against our habit of thinking unhappy thoughts. We are attacking our enemy when we:

*Think about all* we *can praise God for and be glad about.* (Phil. 4:8)

Jesus never sinned in thought, word or deed, yet Satan tried to trick Him into displeasing God. So we can be sure that Satan will also try to trick us in every way possible.

Judas betrayed Jesus. Peter denied Jesus three times. Judas wept and *thought* about his guilt until he ended up hanging himself. Peter repented and received God's forgiveness.

We sometimes wallow in our guilt over our sin and suffer endlessly. When we do that, Satan wins. When we ask for and receive God's forgiveness, His joy and peace replace the horrible burden of guilty thoughts. When we cling to guilt over our past sins, we don't allow God to forgive us – and *He wants* to forgive us. I'm emphasizing this because I hear from so many people who, like Judas, keep clinging to their guilt.

No matter how we have sinned Satan whispers, "You do not deserve to be forgiven or to have great joy." That may seem logical to us, but *it is a lie*.

Because we are God's children, we deserve to be treated in whatever way He desires. And it is *His will* that we receive forgiveness whenever we ask it of Him. God declares that when we confess our sins and truly repent, we are forgiven from that moment forward.

The name Gloria Swanson may not be familiar

to you, but at one time she was the queen of Hollywood. She was wined and dined by celebrities from all over the world. Gloria visited Mary and me at our home in Escondido. She had called to ask if we could help her understand how to become a Christian.

We met with her, and I came to realize how difficult her life had been. As a star in the early days of movie making, Gloria had all the thrills of public acclaim. She made more money than 99% of the U.S. population. She could afford many luxuries, and people from nearly every walk of life sought her company. Her life was a whirlwind of parties and a continual search for happiness. But Gloria said she fell into nearly endless unhappiness. She was overwhelmed with unhappy thoughts. She wanted to know if Jesus could do anything for her.

We explained the simple plan of salvation: faith in Jesus as Savior. The next Sunday Gloria attended the church Mary and I had started in Escondido. At the closing invitation, she came forward to publicly receive Jesus as her Savior.

Gloria ordered hundreds of copies of *Prison to Praise* when she went back to New York, and as a humble servant of her Lord, she stood on street corners giving them away. She often found a way to tell people how she came to know joy for the very first time, when she recognized Jesus as her Lord.

I heard from her occasionally after that. Sometimes she had questions, but usually she wanted to say how glad she was to have met the One who had made her feel loved and accepted. She was elated over how completely God had forgiven all her sins.

Our memories of past mistakes can give us great pain, but Jesus takes our past and converts it into the joy of sins forgiven!

Chapter 8
# *One Million and One*

*A cheerful heart does good like medicine . . . .*
(Prov. 17:22)

Picture a person with a damaged heart, bedfast twenty-four hours a day. They are expected to die unless a new heart can be found. Then one is found! The implant is successful and the person is soon living a new life.

Try to imagine how happy that person would be. They would shout, "I can walk, work, and laugh! I'm alive!" You would be happy for that person, but not having shared their experience, you wouldn't know *how elated* they would be.

Similarly, we read in God's Word:

*You can keep going no matter what happens—always full of the joy of the Lord . . . .* (Col. 1:11)

We may be only mildly thankful for that promise because it seems so foreign to us. We also read:

*Heart, body, and soul are filled with joy.* (Ps. 16:9)

We wonder what could cause such an experience. The following verse offers some insight into what may cause "filled-with-joy" experiences:

*I am always thinking of the Lord; and because he is so near, I never need to stumble or to fall.* (Ps. 16:8)

When we dwell on happy thoughts, they work in us like medicine. Such thoughts may not immediately transform us, but like good medicine they will eventually work good in us.

Of course, a mind that has been *trained* to think unhappy thoughts does not want to be controlled by faith. It whines, "I want to be cheerful but I don't know how."

Even if you haven't been the person you believe God wants you to be, you can find new joy as you discover that God has given you the ability to guide your thoughts.

The things we do today will affect us tomorrow, even if we wish it were not so. For example, what we eat and drink today may affect the way we feel tomorrow, and perhaps for many days to come. Our habits determine who and what we will be for years to come.

Suppose a boy decides he wants to become a basketball star and carries a basketball wherever he goes. His brain, muscles and nerves become focused on how to handle the basketball. He is being shaped and changed, and may eventually become a star.

We, too, can focus our attention on the person we want to become. We can decide NOW that we will rejoice in whatever God allows to come to us. We can "carry" that attitude with us for minutes or hours. We can pick it up so often that, like the boy with a basketball, every part of our being gradually gets the point. Our minds begin to understand the reason for our existence. Our purpose is to believe that God is *always* working for our good. The mind slowly, but surely, grasps the plan. It will not "drop the ball." We can learn to keep our attention focused on trusting God, rather than complaining.

God designed His plan for us, and it works. It may take us a while to understand it, and then another while to learn how to practice it, but as His joy takes root in our hearts it becomes a treasure more valuable than all the riches of the world. His medicine is powerful!

Joy, and ever-increasing joy, is God's plan for us. If we say, "I'll change my attitude when God changes my situation," we will continue to be unhappy people. Nevertheless, some unhappy folks still ask themselves, "Why is my life so unhappy? Why does everything go wrong?" Their attention is so fixed on unhappy things that they seem unable to change their attitude. My hope is that if you are an unhappy person, this book will inspire you to believe that you can become the joyful person that God wants you to be.

We know that our thoughts change us. That being so, what good thoughts might lift us to a happiness that is beyond anything we have yet experienced? Our Creator tells us to be happy, and He also tells us *how* to be happy. Look again at Psalm 16:8: *I am always thinking of the Lord . . . .*

What is it about thinking of the Lord that brings joy and prevents fear? We are told to rejoice in the Lord always, but rejoice in what? Perhaps we rejoice in the good things He gives us. But if only that, how can we rejoice if we end up in prison or placed in an arena to be fed to the lions? No, we must rejoice in His love for us. We will never rejoice in Him more than we do now until we come to know His love for us – really believe He loves us. Then we'll have a clearer understanding of what He wants to *do* for us, and we will love Him all the more.

As humans, we are naturally very happy when we believe that someone loves us. The stronger that belief, the greater our joy. So, too, as we understand God's love for us we will be *filled with joy*!

Knowing that God loves us gives us a remarkable power over fear and pain. But knowing that He loves us isn't enough; we must love Him back:

*Love the Lord your God with all your heart and with all your soul and with all your mind and with all your strength.* (Mark 12:30 NIV)

One of the ways that we can express our love to God is by being thankful. Thankfulness is a natural result of believing that God loves us. When we dwell on these things – God's love for us and our thankfulness to Him – we are happier people.

I am gradually learning how *powerful* thankful thoughts are. They make us feel better and better until we are surprised by how we are changing into happier people. We may not even be able to explain *why* we are feeling so good. Be aware of, and think on, the many things that you can be thankful for. Each new discovery will add to your joy.

We will not be happy in this world until we learn the power of rejoicing in God's goodness. We will never understand His goodness until we *practice* what He tells us to do:

*Give thanks in all circumstances, for this is God's will for you in Christ Jesus.* (1 Thes. 5:18 NIV)

Remember: practice being thankful until it is as

automatic as breathing. You will see results! God rewards our thanksgiving. We can give thanks for an hour and not repeat ourselves. I cannot overemphasize the importance of obeying God until that becomes your way of life.

Thoughts that produce joy and better health are not easy to maintain. Our enemy is an expert in encouraging unhappy thoughts. He knows that if we understand that God wants us to be happy, we will love Him even more. When we *really* know that He loves us, we will want others to know Him too. We will enjoy serving Him and even be willing to give our lives to please Him. Our enemy will do anything to prevent such "disastrous" things from happening!

The problem some of us have is that we spend our lives thinking of things we are *unhappy* about. They may only be small things, but those small things add up. The good news is that our joyful thoughts can add up too – just like grains of sand.

Place a grain of sand on the ground; it is almost invisible. Two grains are nearly the same. Keep adding one at a time and eventually you'll see a small pile of sand. Even a small pile will not have a big effect on anyone. But add enough grains of sand and you'll have a beach that many people can enjoy. As our joyful thoughts keep multiplying, we begin to notice the results – and other people are attracted!

As we learn to mature into greater happiness and contentment, we become enthusiastic representatives of God's Good News. This is what Jesus exhorted His followers to do:

*He told them, "You are to go into all the world and preach the Good News to everyone, everywhere."* (Mark 16:15)

Are you overwhelmed by this mission? Are you discouraged by what seems to be the impossibility of experiencing joy for yourself? You need not be. It all starts with just one happy thought, one grain of sand. Keep practicing, and before long there will be one million and one grains of sand!

## Chapter 9
### *Pleasing God*

Temptation to displease God, and to surrender the joy that He wants us to have, began in the Garden of Eden. Satan tempted Eve:

To look.

To listen.

To think.

Eve *looked* at the forbidden fruit; looking can be with our eyes, or by creating pictures in our minds.

Eve *listened* to Satan's tempting words; we listen to words that come to our ears or to our minds. Both are effective.

Eve *thought* about the forbidden fruit and decided to eat it; looking with desire and *thinking* about those desires will nearly always lead us to the act. Later we like to think, "I just couldn't help myself." We know that isn't true, but we like to find some excuse – just as Adam and Eve tried to excuse themselves before God.

An example of temptation for we men is seeing a woman dressed in a way that leads us to think lustful thoughts. But seeing is not *looking*. We see, and then we decide what we will do next. If we decide to continue looking – or to continue thinking

– even a second longer, that will stimulate more thoughts that we should not have. Jesus said:

*Anyone who looks at a woman lustfully has already committed adultery with her in his heart.* (Mt. 5:28 NIV)

Notice that Jesus used the word *look*. We see homes, cars, food, and many other things that tempt us. If we know that they tempt us, we should not permit ourselves to *look* at or think about them. Remember: see, but don't look!

God's directions to Adam and Eve were clear. He gave them only one *Thou shalt not*: do not eat any fruit from the tree that is in the middle of the garden. Why? You will suffer.

Adam and Eve must have studied the forbidden fruit tree and asked themselves, "Why would God tell us to never eat any of that fruit? It doesn't *look* evil. What harm could it do?"

Then Satan interjected his thoughts on the matter. His lies about why God had forbidden them to eat from that specific tree convinced Eve that she should at least give it a try.

Later God decided that men and women needed more *Thou shalt nots*, so He gave them the Ten Commandments – carved in stone by His own hand! That should have settled the matter. But it didn't. It wasn't long before men and women were breaking His written commandments.

God used an assortment of punishments to teach men that it would be better for them to obey Him. He sent floods, storms, droughts, diseases, wars and poverty. But no form of chastisement dissuaded people from doing what they wanted, when they wanted.

So Jesus came with a new message from God – His solution. He offered complete forgiveness for our sins and the free gift of eternity in Heaven. He said that we should believe in and trust Jesus as our Savior, rather than trying to earn salvation by our own righteousness.

Remember: eternal life and joy are given to those who *believe* Jesus – not to those who *deserve* Him.

Did you know that worry is also displeasing to God? After Adam sinned, he was afraid of God and tried to hide. Being afraid may seem natural, but fear is the result of not trusting God. Worry and fear may seem as acceptable to us as eating fruit from the forbidden tree did to Adam and Eve! But Jesus tells us:

*Do not worry about your life, what you will eat or drink; or about your body, what you will wear.* (Mt. 6:25 NIV)

Martha is an example of how worry can get in the way, even when our intentions are good. Martha wanted to serve Jesus and to do it well. But she also wanted her sister Mary to be as "righteous" as she was. Mary had her own idea about what she should do, and that annoyed Martha. Jesus told Martha that she was troubled about many things and that Mary had done better by simply listening to Him.

His message to you and me is the same:

*Do not be anxious about anything* . . . . (Phil 4:6 NIV)

Worry and fear cling to us, pull us downward, and destroy the joy that God wants us to have. Whatever defective habits we have developed will require much determination and faith to overcome. If, like Adam and Eve, we don't persevere, we, too, will move away from the happiness that God has planned for us. We will cry with the millions before us, "Oh, if only I hadn't done that!"

Every day I receive letters from people who express grief over their past. Some of the stories are heartbreaking because entire families have suffered for the mistakes of an individual.

Remember, even though Satan *desires* to

control what you think, *you decide* whether you will continue to be troubled over your past mistakes or rejoice over God's goodness to you. You decide!

Jesus demonstrated in His own life what it means not to be anxious:

*Jesus was asleep at the back of the boat with his head on a cushion. Frantically they wakened him, shouting, "Teacher, don't you even care that we are all about to drown?" Then he rebuked the wind and said to the sea, "Quiet down!" And the wind fell, and there was a great calm! And he asked them, "Why were you so fearful? Don't you even yet have confidence in me?"* (Mark 4:38-40)

What an illustration! We need confidence, not in our own goodness or strength, but in *Jesus.*

We easily become worried or frightened when we feel like we're about to drown in our problems. To know the peace that Jesus had, we must learn to believe that God will take care of our problems. An unbelieving world may see God as hardhearted or uncaring – just as the disciples saw Jesus when they asked him, *Don't You care?* Of course God cares. That's why He has made provision for us.

We can believe in Christ as our Savior, and then believe in Him even more strongly. Our growing faith causes our joy to increase! We soon want everyone in the world to receive the news that the angel gave to the shepherds:

*Don't be afraid! . . . I bring you the most joyful news ever announced, and it is for everyone!* (Luke 2:10)

Once the reality of this verse sinks deeply into our hearts, we will want to give our lives to help others understand that Heaven is a free gift – given to us because of God's goodness, not our own. Jesus said:

*No one is good—except God alone.* (Mark 10:18 NIV)

I strongly recommend that you thank God that you *are* going to Heaven. Think about your salvation, and thank God for it until it becomes rooted in your heart as one of your core beliefs. This is part of the foundation of your trust in everything that Jesus said! Believing in Him is your hope, your confidence, and your joy!

Jesus said that He is *the way, the truth and the life* (John 14:6). When we tell people what Jesus has done for us, we are serving God – just as Jesus commanded (see John 20:21). This is one way to please God!

To accept Christ's invitation to be His messenger, we need to serve Him as best we know how. He said:

*We can be mirrors that brightly reflect the glory of the Lord.* (2 Cor. 3:18)

God pours His blessings on those who volunteer to serve Him. For the past two thousand years, God has blessed men and women who were enthusiastic. These individuals demonstrated their faith in Jesus by their zeal to help others believe in Him.

Oftentimes I simply ask individuals if they are going to Heaven. Their answers reveal how certain they are. "I hope so," reveals uncertainty. They may mean to indicate that they don't think they are better than other folks. But that is a mistake! No one is "good enough." We are all totally dependent upon God's grace, manifested by Jesus' willingness to pay our penalty. That is the Good News of the Gospel!

When you tell people that you are going to Heaven, your face and your eyes will shine with the joy that Jesus came to bring. Others will be attracted *to Him*! God wants us to feel and look as if being a Christian is the best thing that has ever happened to us, because it is!

Jesus is the only perfect man this world has known. No others, ever. Is that bad news or good news? Good news! Why? Because we all have equal standing before God to receive His Son as our Redeemer and to enjoy what He came to give us!

We may be tempted to think of others as more qualified to serve God than we are. When thinking of those in Christian history who did great things for God, we may consider their spiritual gifts to be way beyond our own. But how could they possibly be more blessed by God than we are? We are all *equal* in His sight. The only difference is that these others permitted God to work in them and change them. If Paul had not allowed God to change him, much of the New Testament would not have been written.

Adam refused to allow God to run his life. You and I have the freedom to do the same. We can choose to displease God. Or, we can choose to please Him. We can permit God to work in and through us, serving in the way He has designed us to serve. If we do, He will help us fulfill His promise to bring the *good news of great joy* to those who do not yet believe in His Son.

Each of us can be God's messenger for this day and for this hour. Whether we have one year, one month or one day left on earth, God can work great things in and through us. All He needs is willing vessels that He can fill with His Spirit!

## Chapter 10
### *Learning To Believe*

How can we please God? Work harder? Pray harder? Give more? Live more holy lives? Wrong answers. God's heroes made their way to the top of His "Most Pleasing to God" list by *having faith in Him*!

Consider the benefits of becoming more pleasing to God. If we do this, we will be far more likely to enjoy answered prayers – for others and for ourselves!

What would you like God to do for you?

God told Noah to build an ark that may have taken him one hundred years to complete. But doing the work wasn't Noah's biggest challenge. He had to believe that God knew what He was doing; even when there was no evidence that an ark would be needed – ever.

Try to imagine what it would be like if you were a 100-year-old man or a 90-year-old woman and God asked you to believe that you were going to have a child. That's what happened to Abraham and Sarah. Think how you would feel if He told you to sacrifice that child on an altar.

Would you be willing to tell over a million people by faith, like Moses did, that you would help them walk through the Red Sea on dry ground – while being pursued by an enemy intent on killing them?

Paul was chained in prison for years, yet never doubted God's perfect goodness. Would you?

In the United States God isn't asking us to walk through fire – yet – but He does ask us to trust Him. It might help us to remember the heroes of the Old Testament. When they trusted God in spite of their situation, they received His praise. We are blessed beyond measure to live when and where we do, but our calling is still *to believe* that God is working for our good – no matter what happens to us. Yes, sometimes that is very difficult, especially when we see no evidence that God is involved. But the more difficult it is to believe, the greater the joy we receive as we refuse to doubt Him.

God values our faith in Him *far above* any good work we do. Salvation itself is based on our faith rather than our good works.

Abraham believed that God would do what He promised, and his faith did not waver. You and I have the same opportunity to *believe* that God is working for *our* good. We have the chance to do this many times every day!

Think of it: every day we have opportunities

to refuse to doubt God! Believing is often difficult, just as it was difficult for Abraham. We, too, are tempted to doubt, but we can – like Abraham – learn to believe.

How many times a day are you tempted to believe that God is not involved in what is happening to you? That is the same number of times you can believe that He *is* involved. He has placed this wonderful truth right in front of us. Our challenge is to expect God to work good in and through our circumstances at all times, and to never look back. With this confidence we can always be increasing in joy.

When we struggle with a problem and want to believe that God is working for our good in our situation, we are tempted to think, "If God will work for my good in just this *one* problem then I will trust Him forever." His response to us is:

*If we must keep trusting God for something that hasn't happened yet, it teaches us to wait patiently and confidently.* (Rom. 8:25)

So, we must trust God for what *hasn't happened yet*. When will He answer our prayers? That is the question we must learn not to ask. If we learn to follow this difficult rule, we open wide the door for

Him to always do what is the *very best* for us. God's best is always best! Learning this brings great joy to His people.

Our flesh always wants *proof.* But God rewards our *faith.* Remember, the more difficult our situation, the greater our opportunity is!

When we face problems it is often difficult to see that anything good could come out of our situations. God asks us to take a step of faith by believing what may seem to be impossible:

*We can rejoice, too, when we run into problems and trials for we know that they are good for us—they help us learn to be patient.* (Rom. 5:3)

Yes, we can rejoice! That is part of our learning to be patient. Paul, who wrote those words, believed that his problems and trials were good for him and were helping him learn to be patient. As you probably know, problems tend to have the opposite effect on us. How your problems affect you depends on whether or not you **believe God is working for your good in the midst of your trials**.

In order to have joy *now* we need to believe *now* that God is in the process of making our problems work for our good. We all know that good things increase our joy. That means that before our joy increases, we have to *recognize* that something is good. We can believe that something is good, even when we can't see the good, because we know that God is at work.

No, it is not always easy to believe and to wait patiently. But we can learn. Consider the reward of learning: joy for ourselves and for those we want to help!

During my sixty-plus years of ministry, a number of people told me that they had tried to believe in God, but had not seen enough evidence to convince them that the Bible is true. When I asked them what they had done to try and believe, they had weak answers in every case. They knew very little about the Bible, had read few books that might help them to believe, and had spent very little time praying for God's help.

People have told me before, with good intentions, that they would "try" praising God for everything to "see if it did any good." Some came to the conclusion that praising God didn't work after all. For how long, I wonder, did they "try" praising God? Both Noah and Abraham had to believe God and trust Him for many, many years. When people told Jesus they would believe Him *if* He showed them a miracle right then, He did *nothing* for them. That is often His reaction when we don't trust Him.

79

Jesus asked the blind to believe, and when they did, He healed them! He encouraged *everyone* to believe that He could help them.

Jesus' disciples trusted Him because they believed He wanted what was best for them. Yet Jesus knew they would die painful deaths. How could that possibly work great good for them?

Not long after Jesus' resurrection from the dead, the disciples went from place to place telling people they had seen Jesus – alive – after He had been crucified. They refused to stop spreading this amazing account and were willing to die rather than renounce what they knew to be true. Their willingness to die for what they believed caused many people to put their faith in Christ.

Now you and I have the opportunity to learn what it means to trust in and rely on everything Jesus said.

We have the incredible, God-given ability to grow in our faith (see 2 Cor. 10:15). Some folks have become so filled with the joy of trusting Jesus that they act like little children. They just overflow with joy.

The disciples asked Jesus who would be greatest in the Kingdom of Heaven (see Mt. 18:1). With a child on His lap, Jesus told them they could not even *enter* the Kingdom unless they became like little children. The child may have been laughing at the time, as little ones are often prone to do. I have read that the average child laughs 400 times a day. I receive joy when someone says to me, "Merlin, you look so happy." To me, that means I am acting like "a little child."

God offers each of us the same child-like joy, and our joy will draw more people to Christ! If we dwell on our problems and failures, we will draw few people – if anyone – to Christ.

You may still be wondering *how* you can learn to have faith that results in joy. Have you picked up a Bible lately? Here is a book that claims to have the answers to life's biggest questions, a book that promises us power and, yes, joy. We should study this book! We should underline special parts, meditate on them, and do our best to determine what *action* to take. This is especially true when we find doubt or unhappiness taking root in our lives. Jesus told us:

*My purpose is to give life in all its fullness.* (John 10:10)

We should examine, learn and practice every-thing Jesus said in order to determine what He meant by *life in all its fullness.* I believe it means joy for all of God's children!

Many people have learned that the more we practice what He taught us, the greater our joy becomes!

## Chapter 11
### *I Don't Want To*

"I don't want to," is a thought that I've thought a million times. We learned that sentiment before we could even talk.

For years I suffered from a glitch in my back. About twice a year I would bend over and WHAM, something would happen that would cause me days of agonizing pain. I heard that I should try stretching exercises before I got out of bed.

The exercises worked, and I didn't have the "wham" problem for several years. Then, when Mary and I were on a vacation. I decided not to bother with the exercises. That decision seemed logical to me. Besides, *I didn't want* to do them.

After a few days, I bent over to pick something up, and the glitch hit me again. There went the vacation.

From then on I listened to a wiser voice: "Do the exercises regardless of how you feel." Later, I learned another important lesson.

I learned to exercise with joy! In fact, I learned to *exercise joy* – joy that I could do the exercises at all, joy that they would do me good, and joy that God was helping me to *rejoice always*. This has made painful stretch exercises enjoyable!

Another important lesson I've learned is that when I first wake up, I can choose my thoughts. For most of my life I've felt driven to get everything done yesterday. So my mind wants to latch onto the things I think should be done right away. And if I'm going to get them done, I need to get busy right away. As soon as I finish one project, my mind immediately goes to the next project. If I start a day feeling pressured, I will probably follow that same manner of thinking the entire day.

God wants me to begin my day with thoughts of praise; work should not be my first priority. A happy heart will prepare us for all the work that *needs* to be done.

*The important thing for us as Christians is . . . stirring up goodness and peace and joy from the Holy Spirit.* (Rom. 14:17)

Notice that we can stir up joy!

The Holy Spirit will help us have thoughts that create joy, not frustration. Keep practicing thankfulness: thank You, God, that I can move my fingers, my arms, my legs and my toes. I can see – what a joy! I can hear! I can breathe and speak! The list is endless. That is precisely why the Bible tells us we can rejoice all the time.

We may say, "*I don't want to* rejoice," but rejoicing is what prepares us for the problems that come. This helps me understand why Satan strives to keep us from learning the secret of rejoicing in the Lord.

Satan wants us to concentrate on what we *don't want to do* and on what we *don't have*. For example, we say, "I don't have enough time!" That kind of thinking will not increase the amount of time we have. We have merely wasted more time.

Or, suppose you can't pick up a one hundred pound weight. It will not help you to dwell on what you *cannot* do. God designed us such that we need to pick up ten-pound weights before we have the strength to pick up a twenty-pound weight. We continue *doing what we can* until eventually we can pick up the one hundred pound weight. It doesn't matter whether or not we want to do it this way. That's the way it is in life. We must do what we can until we can do something more difficult, or else we will miss out on what God has for us because we never get beyond where we are now.

Jesus told the man who couldn't walk:

*Get up! Pick up your mat and walk.* (John 5:8 NIV)

Imagine the man responding, "I don't want to."

Now notice the sequence: get up, pick up, walk. We need to do what we can, and then concentrate on praising God for what we *can* do! No more worrying over what we *cannot* do. That attitude will get us nowhere. The Bible tells us to do such things as clap our hands, sing and rejoice. We can create new attitudes!

Start your day by praising and thanking God. Don't stay in the rut of saying, "I don't want to," because when you exercise a new attitude of praise and thanks, your joy will *increase*. Other people will see your joy and will want the joy that you have. If they ask you about it, you can tell them about the Source of your joy. If we pay attention to what people say to us, we will find many opportunities to tell them about Jesus and what He has done for us.

If you see an unhappy person in a wheelchair, you do not want to ask them why they are sad. But if they seem joyful, you begin to think, "Why are they so happy?" If you are bold enough to ask them, they might tell you.

Folks are surprised when hurting people seem to have joy. God wants us to reveal to the world that we have found the secret to joy. That's why He will sometimes let us be in a "wheelchair." You might be enduring a difficult problem right now. Your problem can work great good for you and for others if, in the midst of it, you manifest the joy you have found in Jesus.

*God sometimes uses sorrow in our lives to help us . . . . We should **never regret his sending it**.* (2 Cor. 7:10, emphasis mine)

Again and again my heart swells with wonder and joy as I read what Paul wrote *while he was in prison*. He wasn't resting on soft pillows when he wrote the words that have stirred men's hearts for two thousand years. I believe that God's heart ached as He watched Paul suffer, but God knew that for many years to come, people would be drawn to Jesus by the things Paul was learning and by his amazing faith in God.

When you and I suffer, we, too, can learn to have more joy! As we do, our faith will increase. How could anyone say, "I don't want to," to that?

Some people believe that Christians should not be happy. Their reasoning is that since many people are suffering, we should be weeping with sorrow for all the hurting ones. The problem with that way of thinking is that *God wants* His children to be happy:

*May the God of hope fill you with all joy and peace as you trust in him, so that you may overflow with hope by the power of the Holy Spirit.* (Rom. 15:13 NIV)

**Joy is God's secret weapon!** Joy defeats the weapons that Satan uses to attack us. I do not comprehend why anyone would ever want less than what the Bible calls *glorious joy.*

*Even though you do not see him now, you believe in him and are filled with an inexpressible and glorious joy* . . . . (1 Peter 1:8 NIV)

Here is a personal question: do you believe that you have *glorious joy* – the kind of joy that might help you lead another person to Christ? If not, Jesus said:

*Ask, and you will be given what you ask for. Seek, and you will find. Knock, and the door will be opened.* (Mt. 7:7)

Remember that no matter how much joy we have, Satan is plotting to steal it. He uses subtle but effective tactics. These tactics, or "joy robbers," are used against the rich and the poor, the sick and the healthy, the weak and the powerful. Has Satan found a way to rob you?

A few of these joy robbers are:

Illness – You may think, "Of course, anyone is unhappy when they are ill." Not so. Some extremely ill people radiate joy. How do they do that? They have learned wonderful truths about joy that often are learned only by those suffering from an illness.

Poverty – The enemy hopes that this tactic will work on those who have always been poor, as well as on those who have had wealth but lost it. Still, some folks who are poor radiate joy.

The Weather – No matter how wet or dry, hot or cold it is, some people feel miserable. But many folks have learned to have joy in *any* weather.

Old Age – Some older folks have more joy than the rest. My Aunt Mimi is a good example. She is in her 90's, nearly blind, and lives alone. When people need to be cheered up, they call her! She tells me that she learned long ago to be cheerful no matter what was going on in her life. That is what she chooses to be! Now she is enjoying to the fullest what she has learned.

You can probably think of other things that cause people to lose their joy. But no matter what the problem is, Jesus is always the solution. Jesus believed God, and because He believed, God answered His prayers. You and I haven't learned to believe as effectively as Jesus did, but we can learn to believe more than we do now.

We learn to solve problems by our faith – not by becoming unhappy. I once saw myself as a very unhappy person, and I could list all the reasons *why* I was unhappy. And, I felt, if God were real He would do something to help me. But God loved me too much to just give me what I thought I needed. He wanted to help me learn to believe Him.

I *began* to learn, and although it was slow and difficult, God didn't give up on me. Eventually I came to believe I was the happiest person alive! That is what I still believe and that is who I am today. Now I want to help other Christians to join me!

# Chapter 12
## *Any Complaints?*

God wants us to experience His joy in an ongoing, consistent way. So why isn't that our reality?

Although God tells us to rejoice in Him always (see Phil. 4:4), we have the freedom to receive or reject that command. Christians believe that Jesus is the Son of God, but many have not laid claim to the strength and joy that He offers. God, through the work of His Son and by means of His Holy Spirit, offers us His incomparable joy – but He will not force it upon us. The choice is ours. Any complaints so far?

We daily choose between belief and unbelief. Belief is characterized by faith and the joy that comes from faith, while unbelief is characterized by an ill temper, judging of others, and complaining. Which have you chosen today?

An ill temper is the opposite of joy. God absolutely does not want His children to engage in anything that will not bring His joy. An ill or bad temper is often considered a harmless weakness, not to be considered too seriously. But we are called to be loving, and the Bible says very clearly:

*Love . . . is not irritable or touchy.* (1 Cor. 13:5)

If we were to add up the results of irritable and touchy tempers, we would discover far more suffering than we may have expected. Marriages, families, churches and even businesses are destroyed because of ill tempers. And there is an even graver result:

*Your souls aren't harmed by what you eat, but by what you think and say!* (Mark 7:15)

Here's another stern word:

Do not judge, and you will not be judged. . . . (Luke 6:37 NIV)

Judging others decreases our own happiness! It is easy for us to condemn others so frequently that we become unaware that we are doing it! We think of things that our spouses, children or friends do that we do not like. They may be small flaws, but if we meditate on their imperfections, each thought drains away part of our joy.

If you want to test this, spend five minutes thinking about all the things you wish people would not do. When you finish you will not be overflowing with joy. Now try the opposite. Spend five minutes thinking about all the things you *like* about people. Notice the difference!

Dwelling on the good in others leaves no room for complaining. And we are prone to complain. Our grumbling, anxiety and unhappiness are encouraged by the fallen, broken world in which we live. These things may seem to be a normal, natural part of being human, but they are not what God designed us for.

Remember that every organ of the body thrives on joy – not unhappiness! We were designed for joy, and in eternity we will live in joy. That is God's plan for us. So if we want to be a part of what God *wants* to do in all His children, we can begin NOW – and continue tomorrow.

Am I putting too much emphasis on our seemingly natural tendencies to complain? Let's consider God's attitude:

*Don't murmur against God and his dealings with you, as some of them did, for that is why God sent his Angel to destroy them.* (1 Cor. 10:10)

When the Israelites wandered in the desert, they began to complain. How did God respond? *He sent His Angel to destroy them.* What happened there in the desert is important to us because we are so prone to do the same things the Israelites did:

*All these things happened to them as examples—as object lessons to us—to warn us against doing the same things; they were written down so that we could read about them and learn from them . . . .* (1 Cor. 10:11)

Thousands of people were destroyed because they *murmured* (grumbled and complained). The Jews thought that living in the dry, dusty, miserable desert gave them license to grumble. By the time they left the desert, many thousands had died because they complained and did not trust God. Now, do you have any complaints?

The Israelites' experience in the desert was reported as evidence that certain attitudes are *not acceptable* to God.

I served for fifty-five years as a pastor and Army Chaplain, speaking and ministering throughout the U.S. and in many foreign countries. Those experiences helped me learn how crucial our attitudes are. If we approach God with the wrong attitude we will not get the response we desire.

With the right attitude we can possess the joy that God promises to give us. God describes this attitude:

*Enter his gates with thanksgiving and His courts with praise.* (Ps. 100:4 NIV)

The results of everything we do depend on our attitude. While people notice what we do, they are far more likely to observe our attitude – be it good or bad. If we change our attitude, people respond with, "Hey, that person is different!"

Having the right attitude toward God may mean serving Him differently than you do now. Do you feel like cringing when you are exhorted to serve God more? That's understandable because in our culture we often feel rushed and hurried. But God may not want us to spend more *time* in serving Him. He may want us to change the *way* we serve Him.

People may ask for more of our time, but what they often want is evidence that we really care about them. They may want our *attitude* to change.

We greet people in many different ways, and each greeting has a completely different effect. If we merely glance at someone and then move on to something else, that person may feel that we barely noticed them. On the other hand, we can fix our attention on a person and make them feel that we want to communicate with them. We notice when someone gives us their attention!

When we worship God, we either give Him our attention or we absent-mindedly use our voices while our hearts and minds think of other things. When we are finished "worshiping" we may not remember what was said or done. When our prayers, singing, giving, and participation in worship are centered in Our Father, He knows it! He responds by giving us His joy.

Jesus came to bring us joy. He provides the Holy Spirit to help us escape the heavy burdens that Satan tries to thrust upon us. The devil knows that if he can make us unhappy, we risk the same sufferings that came to the Israelites.

How do we receive Jesus' joy?

Jesus taught His disciples to believe God and receive gifts from Him. After He left, they continued to believe and work miracles in His name. They recorded their experiences so that we, too, might learn to believe. Everything we need to know about living joyful, victorious lives is found in the Bible – right at our very fingertips! Still, the choice is ours. We must choose to believe.

The Bible makes some bold statements that we may struggle to believe. For example, we tend to read Paul's amazing guidelines to spiritual victory and dismiss or dilute what he says. Why? Because his statements appear to contradict all that we have seen or experienced. *Rejoicing in the Lord always* seems like an impossible goal. *Not being anxious about anything* strikes us as childish. Thinking about only those things which are *pure, admirable, excellent or praiseworthy* appears impractical in the real world. But we do indeed wish that we could have *the peace of God that is beyond our understanding* (see Phil. 4:7)!

Christ's most important gift of salvation requires believing Him! Then we can continually strengthen what we already believe. We see evidence in the lives of many people that believing in and relying on Jesus is the only known way to enjoy life and be unafraid of death. I have faced death many times, and each occasion has proven to me that my faith in Jesus has prepared me both to live and to die.

Our attitude is so very important:

*Be made new in the attitude of your minds . . . .* (Eph. 4:23 NIV)

Practice believing, and believing, and believing. Unbelief cultivates an ill temper and complaining, but belief brings joy.

Have faith! The call of both the Old and New Testaments is, **"Have faith!"** God's unchanging instruction for His children is to have faith in Him. God designed us, and He knows exactly what will help us.

Suppose a doctor tells you that because of your weakened health it is crucial that you walk one mile a day. "Fair enough, I'll walk one mile a day," you say. After a few days you don't feel like doing the entire mile, so you shorten the distance to half a mile. Feeling comfortable, you later make it a quarter mile. Soon you decide to give up walking altogether. Eventually you can't walk at all. It happens to people all the time.

Our Spiritual Doctor says, "Rejoice always." We say, "Fair enough. I'll rejoice all the time." Then we find one thing, only one, that we cannot rejoice about. We accept that. Later we find another thing that we simply can't rejoice about. Then we find more things that we cannot – absolutely cannot – rejoice about. In time, we become unhappy people. Why? Because we did not follow our Great Physician's directions. It happens to people all the time.

We weaken our faith when we decide God is not using something to bless us. When such pronouncements are made over and over, they take root deep in our hearts. We do not grow in faith; happiness eludes us; unbelievers are not drawn to Christ.

When we believe that difficult situations will bring us happiness, our faith grows! Jesus was always expecting good things to come out of *everything*. Persecutions, torture, and even crucifixion meant coming victory. He taught us to never be anxious. Have faith! Believe! Rejoice!

You may not be facing serious infirmities or problems right now, but the day will come when you will desperately need faith in God's promises to care for you. Jesus said:

*Have faith in God.* (Mark 11:22 NIV)

And God gave us a powerful way to grow in faith – a way that can be used every moment of every day! It is by believing that God is using every situation to work for our good. After a lifetime of seeing only the *problems* in difficult situations, it is difficult to change. But we can change! We can be more like Jesus!

Jesus laid aside His power and knowledge to become a man (see 2 Cor. 8:9 and Phil. 2:6-8). So often we focus on His wisdom, miracles, and perfect obedience to God, and we forget that He was a human being. Jesus lived, learned, and was tempted, just like other men – only He didn't sin.

*God put into effect a . . . plan to save us. He sent his own Son in a human body like ours—except that ours are sinful—and destroyed sin's control over us by giving Himself as a sacrifice for our sins.* (Rom. 8:3)

And Jesus completed His mission! Jesus won! He won for you and me!

*If death got the upper hand through one man's*

*wrongdoing, can you imagine the breathtaking recovery life makes, sovereign life, in those who grasp with both hands this wildly extravagant life-gift, this grand setting-everything-right, that the one man Jesus Christ provides?* (Rom. 5:17 MSG)

What an inheritance we have! We can claim this benefit: to live as though we know who we really are. How would we act if we truly believed what Jesus said about us?

We can believe that God will honor our testimony for Christ, just as God honored what Jesus said. With that faith we can speak boldly and confidently.

God knows, far better than we do, what His Son did for us. And He will help *anyone* who has zeal to lift up His Son. To accomplish His mission, Jesus:

*Wrapped Himself in zeal as in a cloak.* (Is. 59:17 NIV)

When God looks at you, does He see that you have zeal? Think of it: if you have Christ's zeal, God will see Christ in you. What an opportunity!

Zeal on our part isn't necessary in order to have God's love and forgiveness. But just as Jesus selected certain people with whom He would fellowship, He selects people now to advance God's Kingdom. God tells us:

*Whatever your hand finds to do, do it with all your might . . . .* (Ecc. 9:10 NIV)

Following that guideline helps us with our marriages, our children, our work, and all the relationships in our lives. Are you missing out on the blessing of investing yourself fully, with all your might? Do you find yourself asking, "What's the point?"

Your happiness depends on whether or not you believe your life has purpose. Jesus' life had purpose, but what about ours? When speaking to God, Jesus said:

*As You sent me into the world, I am sending them into the world . . . .* (John 17:18)

What an honor we have been given! Jesus sends us in the *same way* that God sent Him! We have such amazing reasons to rejoice in our calling. Jesus doesn't give us a burden. He gives us the authority to rejoice in what we are called to do!

Jesus went on to explain that He wasn't just talking about the believers living in His day, but about every future believer. To me, this is awesome.

Jesus has sent me into the world just as God sent Him into the world! Then He said:

> *I have given them the glory you gave me . . . .* (John 17:22)

Jesus has given us the glory that God gave Him! We share in His victory, His promises, His calling and His glory! Any complaints?

## Chapter 13
## *Living in Perfect Comfort*

A boy came home after his first day in kindergarten and said to his parents, "I'm sure glad that's over." When they asked what he meant, he said, "I'm glad I don't have to go to school again."

"You have to go again tomorrow," they replied.

"But you told me that if I went to school I'd grow up to be smart. I went to school, so now I'll grow up to be smart."

When we become Christians we have new life in Christ. We may want to enjoy all the benefits without doing the things Jesus taught us, but new life with Christ means following Him and learning to do what *He* wants us to do. This is our pathway to ever-increasing joy.

Just as we exercise our muscles, we need to:

*Grow in spiritual strength and become better acquainted with our Lord and Savior Jesus Christ.* (2 Peter 3:18)

We either practice being filled with joy as we rejoice in the Lord, or we practice being unhappy and our spiritual strength will gradually decline.

When a great wave of persecution drove believers out of Jerusalem and scattered them as far as 1,000 miles away, spiritual strength was of utmost importance (see Acts 8:1,4). Peter wanted to encourage these Jewish Christians. He wrote to them:

*These trials are only to test your faith, to see whether or not it is strong and pure. It is being tested as fire tests gold and purifies it – and your faith is far more precious to God than mere gold . . . .* (1 Peter 1:7)

You and I are tested in different ways, to see if our faith is strong and pure.

A football coach supplies his team with what they need: work and more work. Practice and more practice. Only then do they have a chance to defeat their opponents. God strengthens us in the same way.

One day believers in Jesus will hear, *Well done, good and faithful servant.* If we believe that we are destined for an eternity that is perfect, we can joyfully follow Jesus' rules for a few years here on earth. If He says to sing when everyone around us is crying, we can. If He says, "Trust Me," when everyone around us doubts, we can trust Him regardless of what is going on. Even in the face of serious illness, let's do our best to believe He is working for our good.

Remember how Jesus pulled Peter out of the water when he was sinking? Peter wasn't sinking because He was a bad person, but because his fear became greater than his trust in Jesus. Jesus is with you and me just as surely as He was with Peter, and He wants us to learn to trust Him.

One day I hope to be able to say with Paul, "I have fought a good fight. I have kept the faith." Now if the Bible said, "Merlin, you *must* be strong and fight a good fight," I would be anxious. I know I am not as strong as I should be. But the Bible says:

*Be strong in the Lord, and in His mighty power.* (Eph. 6:10 NIV)

We can enjoy being *strong in the Lord* and *in His mighty power*! His power is available to us when we **believe Him**.

If we evaluate ourselves by our own abilities, sooner or later we will feel incapable of being what we should be. Many people live with that unhappy, "I'm a failure," feeling. But when we believe Christ's promise to supply whatever we need (see Phil. 4:19), we can believe that God is finding a way to accomplish His will in us.

The glass can either be half empty or half full. Every day we choose how to perceive life. We make that decision so often that it becomes ingrained in us, and we aren't even aware we are making it. But God is aware, and it is important to Him that we learn to trust Him. Without this trust we will never receive the blessings He has reserved for those who trust Him.

If I can only walk one step, I will be tempted to grumble because I cannot walk two steps. If I can walk two steps, I will want to criticize the fact that I can't walk four steps. That is the fallen nature of our human race. We are a complaining people; we have always been so. Our sinful nature drives us to find fault with ourselves and other people. Satan's goal is to get every person to complain about everything.

Jesus is the author of believing and praising God. He came to the world with a message of joy. He said to people: open your eyes; stand up and walk; walk on the water; feed the hungry; heal the sick. He emphasized what we could do *if we believed* (see Mark 9:23).

When threatened, Jesus said He could not be touched unless it was God's will. He refused to be a victim of anything or anyone. On the cross He asked God to forgive those who wanted to kill Him. He died, but not because men wanted to kill

Him. In the Father's timing, Jesus gave His spirit to God and His body died. He was never a victim!

Jesus called you and me to never be victims of people, places, or things. Learn that truth, and you will make a giant step toward understanding how to deal with everything that happens here on earth. God can control sickness, disease, and life itself (see Ps. 139:1-16). When we believe this, we voluntarily place ourselves under His control.

Why then does sickness come upon us?

When sin entered the world, sickness, disease and death (and complaining) also came. When I walk, one foot hurts. Notice I didn't say that my knees and my hips do *not* hurt. We tend to emphasize what hurts. We're sick, we're tired or we're poor. Why? Because we see our glass as half empty. So long as that is our emphasis, our joy and peace will be severely limited. And, our faith *will not* control our lives.

No more groaning or moaning that it's time to get up in the morning. Saying, "Thank You, God, it's time to get up," is an act of faith. When our flesh convinces us to whimper, "Poor me," or, "Oh no, it's time to go to work again," we are being lured into unhappiness. There are so many reasons to be thankful: you have a job, are able to work, and have a roof over your head. Believing God in such simple things may seem to be unimportant, but little things add up to big things.

Jesus taught His disciples the importance of believing that God's best would come to them. He taught them to be unafraid of storms even when their boat began to sink. He wanted them to believe they would not sink, even when they were standing on water. Not sink? How could that be? They had always been pulled down by gravity. But Jesus showed them it could be done.

We may never learn to walk on water, but we can learn how to rejoice in the Lord always. Jesus said we need never sink, regardless of the seemingly irresistible forces that try to pull us down. Let's learn to believe that our glass is always at least half full!

The Bible teaches us how to be victorious in a sinful, fallen world. Scripture says we can run but not be weary. How can that be? He who gets "weary" when running is not thinking of the blessing of being able to run! If we learn to pattern our thinking according to what we *don't have*, we are destined for much unhappiness.

Be aware that when we try to control our thoughts, we enter a fierce spiritual battle. The habit of complaining is a stronghold that Satan does not want to relinquish. Satan wants us to believe that we have no control over our thoughts, because then he has more control. Unfortunately, many people have fallen under the delusion that their particular desire for something is so powerful and controlling that there is nothing they can do – except to want it.

The lure of having and doing what we want does not become overpowering by accident. It happens slowly and by increments. We are not first enticed to do something that is clearly wrong, such as robbing a bank. No! It happens over time. It begins with seemingly unimportant things that we pay little attention to and soon forget. For example, a boy promises his mother that he will take out the trash. At the time, he intends to keep his promise. But then his friends come by, so he decides to go out instead. That's how it is with us. When something becomes inconvenient or unpleasant, we opt for that which is most pleasing to us at the moment.

Doing what *we want* to do easily becomes a lifestyle. Gradually, but surely, we guarantee suffering for ourselves and for others. Unless we are convinced to make a radical change in our decision-making, we dig ourselves into a dark hole.

Another simple illustration is the choices we make regarding what and when we will eat and drink. For many years, our poor choices do not seem to threaten our health and happiness. But then there are warning signs that all is not well.

How do we break the habit of consuming what we think we want? Not easily, as many people will attest!

Breaking habits of any kind usually requires assistance. Perhaps that means reading a book like this one. Without a doubt, all of us need help in learning how to desire *what is best* for us.

We all understand that some thoughts are harmful, or even wrong, but we have become accustomed to *and comfortable with* our own ways of thinking. We may accept this as being natural and honestly believe that we have no control over our thoughts.

It's not wrong to be critical of ourselves, but when self-criticism makes us miserable, we may be interfering with God's plans for us. He wants us to have confidence in Him and joy. And we can, because with Jesus working in us, we can do whatever God asks of us (see Phil. 4:13).

It may take some of us a little longer to reach our goals than it does other folks, but taking longer may give us even greater joy! If our minds are always set on, "God is working for my good," it means that we believe He is taking the abilities He gave us and is helping us to become whatever He designed us to become.

We can rate our comfort zone between 1 and 100, with 100% being perfect comfort. Most of us have never been in the perfect comfort zone; we live around the 50% zone. It is possible for us to move upward, and Jesus came to show us how. Some Christians are stuck in their (glass half empty) level of happiness. They believe that a change in their *situation* is the only way to change how they feel. Satan can sometimes (with God's permission) manipulate our circumstances, but the Bible teaches that it is usually *we* who need to be changed – not our circumstances.

Jesus lived in the perfect zone and He invites us to move closer to Him. Believe it or not, the choice is ours.

Thoughts like, "I'm being mistreated," can be ingrained in our minds and become second nature to us. It's very difficult to be joyful if we feel mistreated. The fact is that there will always be people who mistreat others. But you and I can insulate ourselves from them! We can turn ourselves over to our Creator and, like Jesus, believe that God is 100% in charge of everything *anyone* does to us. Is that too much to hope for? In the natural world, yes. But Jesus opened a supernatural doorway for us. When He stood before Pilate, Jesus said:

*You would have no power over me if it were not given to you from above.* (John 19:11 NIV) (Please read this verse several times)

We don't have the faith that Jesus had, but we can grow in confidence. We can change the way we think about the power other people have over us. For example, if the driver of another vehicle rudely cuts in front of you, you can smile and think, "God permitted you to do that so that I could learn to rejoice and be glad." We can rejoice even as we are trying to understand the benefits Jesus offers us. Paul wrote:

*He has given you the whole world to use, and life and even death are your servants.* (1 Cor. 3:22)

Paul truly believed what he wrote, as evidenced by the way he lived:

*Some Jews . . . turned the crowds into a murderous mob that stoned Paul and dragged him out of the city, apparently dead. But as the believers stood around him, he got up and went back into the city! The next day he left with Barnabas for Derbe.* (Acts 14:19-20)

A murderous mob.
They stoned Paul.
They thought he was dead.
They dragged him out of the city.
He got up. Went back into the city.

He left for Derbe the *next day*.

Talk about practicing what you preach!

Luke, the physician, presents this as an ordinary day in the life of Paul, the man who wrote, *Life and even death are your servants.*

We apparently have much to learn. But even as slow learners we can rejoice in the potential God has given us!

We *can* become the happy people God designed us to be. We can be happier now than we were a few minutes ago, and happier still at every future opportunity!

## Chapter 14
### *Are You In A Rut?*

How do you rate on the "Happiness Scale?" Maybe you don't want to know for fear you wouldn't register favorably. Perhaps you think of yourself as being unhappy, but still try to put on a good face so other people won't notice. If so, you're not alone. Many people put on a happy face and smile a lot, all the while feeling very *un*happy. They wouldn't want others to know how frequently *they* feel unhappy.

Many folks just *know* that if they had the particular thing they desire, they would be happy. Even though they see others who seem to have everything and still aren't happy, they remain convinced that they are the exception to the rule. These unhappy people know *for sure* that if they had "this one thing," they would be rolling in happiness.

Every person is unique, but in many ways we are all the same. At one time or another, we all want to be on "the other side of the fence" where the grass seems to be greener.

If you are on the unhappy side of the fence, there is a way for you to cross over. Jesus opened the door for us to enter the life that God wants for

His children. He said:

I have told you this so that you will be filled
with my joy. Yes, your cup of joy will overflow!
(John 15:11)

I am striving to understand and receive what
Jesus told us. Did He really mean that we could
live on this earth and be filled with His joy?

It must be possible, because His disciples experienced this joy:

*And the disciples were filled with joy and with the
Holy Spirit.* (Acts 13:52 NIV)

Are you filled with joy? Would you like to be?
It may seem to you that this joy is impossibly out
of reach. Maybe you've tried very hard for a long
time to make things change, but everything is the
same. Or maybe you've become discouraged and
have given up on trying to change. Maybe you're
in a rut.

If you are in a rut, you would probably like to
get out. It may be *crucial* for you to escape.

Ruts are easy to get into, but sometimes very
difficult to get out of. Men who have had military
training nearly always step forward on their left
foot. That is a "rut" that has been ingrained in their

minds. They automatically use that foot. Only with considerable effort can they break the habit.

Other habits are far more difficult to break.

I used to catch myself thinking of mistakes I had made in the past. That was my rut. I knew God had forgiven me, but I wondered, "Why did I do such a stupid thing?" This habit caused me to waste time, and I certainly wasn't rejoicing. I've observed that getting older causes many folks to meditate on the bad things that have happened to them. I sometimes find myself thinking about my experience during war times, or other unhappy times. Those thoughts never give me joy.

So now when I'm reminded of mistakes I've made, I quickly redirect my thoughts so that I don't dwell on unhappiness. (I often repeat some of the scripture verses that you have found in this book.)

If we aren't careful, even thoughts about happy times can lead us into unhappy thoughts! Remembering times of joy can trigger the rebellious thought, "But those days are gone forever," and that can drag us down.

Jesus gave us a message that He designed to lift us out of unhappiness. He said:

*Because of your faith it will happen.* (Mt. 9:29)

It is definitely in our best interest to have faith!

Part of having faith is doing the things that we *are able* to do, even while we trust God to work for our good.

Old age creeps up on us and has a way of making us awaken in the morning feeling tired. One morning I lay in bed, eyes closed, wishing it were easier to get up. I began to pray for wisdom to know how to wake up and get out of bed without it being so-o-o-o difficult. As I was praying, a question came to my mind: "Do you think God would answer a prayer like that?"

"No, I don't think He would."

"Why not?"

"I don't know."

Eyes closed, still lying there feeling tired, I remembered one of the prayers that Jesus had answered. He had healed the blind man by telling him to open his eyes.

Jesus often told people to do what they *could* do. I realized that I could lie in bed all day with my eyes closed and feeling tired, or I could open my eyes, hold them open, and get out of bed. Everyone knows that's what we need to do in the morning, but I had been seeking an easier way. Very often we ask God to do things *for* us so life will be *easier*. We want Him to make things less difficult. But I'm convinced that He wants us to do what we are *able* to do so we can receive His joy.

David slew the giant, but how? First he had to find stones, walk toward the giant, and then do what he *could* do to win his battle. That's what life is like for God's children. He offers us joy, but we must do what we can to acquire it. He has enabled us to do so.

Another way that we can exercise faith is by giving thanks. When we think, "I can give thanks for some things, but not for this," we are in a rut. We know it's possible to escape this rut because God tells us:

*Always give thanks for everything to our God and Father in the name of our Lord Jesus Christ.* (Eph. 5:20)

This verse presents a problem. How can I honestly say, "Thank You, God," for something that I'm not thankful for in the least?

Herein lies evidence that God inspired the Bible. He foresaw the problem we might have, so He carefully wrote that we should give thanks *in the name of Jesus.* By adding *in His name*, we confess our inability to always be completely thankful, and we trust that because of Jesus living in us, we are thankful!

Giving thanks for *all* things requires that we

give thanks for one thing, then two things, and then on to many things. When it is difficult for us to walk one step, we must persevere if we hope to one day walk a mile. Eventually, giving thanks to God becomes habitual. It becomes a new "rut" that we are in.

When difficult things happen, our minds can react with, "God is always working for my good." We become more and more conditioned to give thanks, so that our first response is always, "Thank You, God." Then we don't have to wrestle with, "But how is God going to make *that* work for my good?"

I had the opportunity to see this principle working in my own life. I had a stroke, which temporarily caused me to forget how to put words together to form even a simple sentence. But one sentence kept coming to my mind: "God is working for my good." I kept thinking that over and over. As I lay on the hospital bed, that was the only thing I could think of! (I was in a rut.)

As God restored my mind, I became increasingly thankful that I could once again put words into a sentence. Now I rejoice that I am able to think and to use that ability to think good, happy and praiseworthy thoughts.

The fact of the matter is that we don't always *feel* like giving thanks. But our emotions are not good masters. We must learn to be guided by the One who came to teach us, and not by the way we feel. We must surrender our emotions to Him. Though it is sometimes difficult to believe, He *can* give us joy in any situation. Yes, you can have joy in *your* situation, because He has a joy that is designed just for you.

Since the way we *feel* is such an important part of life, we need to learn how God's Holy Spirit can influence our feelings.

We're inclined to think, "I'll do those things when I feel like it, but for now I'll just be the way I am." Don't fall back into that rut! If by our actions we say to those we live with, "I'll be helpful and loving when I feel like it," we are not acting as Jesus did. But if we permit God's joy to work in our hearts, no matter how we feel, we will help the people around us – and ourselves.

There are times when my head, spine, feet and hands gang up on me and say, "We don't feel good today, so it's okay for you to be irritable." If I give in to that impulse, I'm not being a good representative for Christ and I won't feel very joyful.

When you are out walking, try an experiment. Think, "I'm tired," or "I don't feel well," over and over again. Notice how much more tired or badly you feel. Then start thinking, "God is so good," or, "God loves me," and observe how much more joyful you feel. Our thoughts change the way we *feel* and *act*.

It has been a great joy for me to learn to sing when I'm out walking, especially if I feel tired. The more I sing, the more joy I feel. I sing some of the old choruses and hymns that I learned years ago. One old hymn puts it this way:

"I have a song that Jesus gave me / It was sent from heaven above;

There never was a sweeter melody / 'Tis a melody of love.

In my heart, there rings a melody / There rings a melody with heaven's harmony;

In my heart there rings a melody / There rings a melody of love."

If you know the tune, sing it over and over. If you don't, make up your own tune, or sing songs that you do know, or make up your own!

Praising God is one more way that we act in faith. When we praise God, we climb out of the rut of unhappiness. How do we make praising God our new habit? Practice. Lots of practice.

We play a musical instrument by learning the fundamentals and then practicing, day after day. We learn to praise the Lord and to experience the joy He wants to give us by knowing the fundamentals as recorded in the Bible, and then practicing – day after day. The more we learn and practice, the less difficult and more enjoyable our lives become.

Learning to play an instrument is usually difficult. Learning to praise the Lord and to have a joyful heart is also difficult at first, but the Holy Spirit is a patient and faithful teacher.

In my first book, *Prison to Praise*, you can read about the simple exercises that I was taught as I learned how to praise God. I learned more each day, and I'm *still* learning. The more we learn, the more enjoyable God's plan becomes.

Thinking happy thoughts and rejoicing can change our lives. It's not always easy to do, but it carries great rewards!

*The troubles will soon be over, but the joys to come will last forever.* (2 Cor. 4:18)

Christians do not have a problem-free life. But God's joy is His gift to us, *no matter what happens.* That is a victory that Jesus won for us, and as we believe, our hearts learn to sing.

Scripture emphasizes that our fallen, sinful nature tries to pull us downward into unhappiness. But the Holy Spirit wants to lift us up so we can be the joyful people God designed us to be. Every part of our anatomy works best when we are

123

rejoicing in Him. Sing and make melody in your heart. Practice, and keep on practicing; you'll be happily surprised at the results!

God knocked down a few walls that I had built around myself before He convinced me that He was my one, unchanging source of happiness. Then I wanted to convince *everyone* to seek His joy! But not everyone believed me.

Many said, "Merlin has gone off the deep end." There I was, so happy and just wanting to tell someone about it. I began to believe that the impossible was possible! Then God provided ways for me to share His joy with others, ways exceedingly and abundantly greater than I could have ever hoped for. Whatever I believed – and even beyond that – was possible!

Jesus could heal any disease and even raise the dead, but in the presence of unbelief He could not help people.

*Because of their unbelief he couldn't do any mighty miracles among them . . . .* (Mark 6:5)

Think of it: the power of unbelief is so strong that it can prevent even God's Son from doing what He wants to do!

Therefore, we *should learn* to believe God's promises. Believing means having faith, and we already know that growing in faith is hard work. It's easy just to believe in what we can see for ourselves. If I tell a person that I have found great joy in what I believe, they may respond, "Some people will believe anything. Not me. I don't believe anything unless someone proves it to me." *Not believing* is a million times easier than learning to *believe*. It's easier to sit in a rut than to try and climb out.

According to our faith, it will eventually be. We can exercise and declare our faith over and over, every day, until we've climbed out of the rut of unhappiness and unbelief. With faith comes its natural byproduct – JOY!

## Chapter 15
## *No Problem*

You have heard it said in jest: "The devil made me do it." Have you ever been aware of the moments when an evil power is tempting you to do something? You don't hear an audible suggestion – you just feel yourself being drawn to do something wrong.

We sometimes feel guilty even when we have no reason to feel that way. A thief attempts to steal without being detected. Guilty thoughts can come to us in such a subtle way that we aren't even aware they come from an outside source. Sometimes people tell me how guilty they feel even after they have asked God to forgive them. They live in their *guilt* instead of living in Christ's forgiveness.

Satan has been invading men and women's thoughts for thousands of years and he knows the best way to infect our minds – without our realizing it. When Peter reprimanded Jesus for wanting to go to Jerusalem where they might kill Him, Jesus spoke very sternly to Peter because He knew that Satan was actually speaking *through* him. Peter had unknowingly allowed Satan to control his thoughts and therefore he was troubled. Remember that it is

Satan who works to make us feel troubled. Jesus says not to be troubled about anything (see John 14:1).

Sometimes it is easy to recognize thoughts that come from our enemy. For example, have you ever been on a balcony in a tall building and felt the urge to jump off? You had zero desire to commit suicide, but the thought still came to you.

Think of how marvelous it is that we can also have thoughts that come from the Holy Spirit! In the book of Acts the Holy Spirit gave the disciples specific instructions on what they should do. We should also learn how to receive the Spirit's directions since part of His mission is to teach us how to experience the joy that Jesus came to give us.

Jesus knew it would be difficult for us to understand the enormity of what He was giving us, so He encouraged us with this promise:

*When the Holy Spirit, who is truth, comes, he shall guide you into all truth . . . .* (John 16:13)

Do not hesitate to ask the Holy Spirit to guide you.

Jesus came to invite us into a relationship with God that no one had ever enjoyed and would result in a happiness nothing in this world could ever give! He said:

*The words I have spoken to you are Spirit and they are life.* (John 6:63 NIV)

Jesus' words brought sight to the blind and life to the dead, and they provide answers to our questions! The more we understand His words, the greater our joy will become. It may seem natural for us to concentrate on the material world, but then we remain unaware of spiritual powers.

Consider this: we normally see our world from a height of around five to six feet. When you are flying in an airplane you see the world from an altitude of thousands of feet. And if you should ever be so fortunate to ride in a space ship, you would see the world from a completely different perspective.

Jesus saw and understood our world from God's perspective. He knew that spiritual powers are real. He knew that God's joy and peace are not dependent upon anything that is going on around us. If we learn to look at life from His viewpoint we will be able to enjoy more of the blessings that He came to give us.

When I was a young man I expected that every good thing would come to me. When "bad things" came my way, my expectations changed. I saw no reason to rejoice since I wasn't experiencing the life that I wanted.

People did not treat Jesus well; His life was not "fair." But He believed that whatever God planned for Him was best. In fact, He saw everything from a completely different perspective than I once did.

Try to imagine how this world seemed to Jesus. He saw our physical problems from a completely different perspective than we do. When Jesus saw sick people, He did not see them as sick. He saw them as receiving health. He saw the dead as coming back to life. He healed deformity and disease by speaking a word. When He told the dead to come back to life, back to life they came!

Whatever the problem was, Jesus saw it as solved. He saw everything as . . . *no problem.* Can you and I learn to do that? He said we could.

At first His disciples probably thought, "No way can we ever learn to do that." Later, when they learned to hear the voice of the Holy Spirit, they saw the world very much like Jesus did. They began to do miraculous things and wrote the words that would help us trust God. The disciples did learn, just as Jesus believed they would! You and I can also learn to see problems His way. The decision is up to us.

Learning to receive more of God's blessings is comparable to seeing the world from outer space. We can tell others *what* we saw, but they may not understand until they, too, get "out there." Remember, no one gets into space until he finds a vehicle to take him there. Jesus' words are our vehicle.

Jesus told us to **never be troubled about anything** (see John 14:27). For many of us, that is a starting point.

At one time, it seemed to me that life on earth was a big mistake. Why should I live when everything seemed so hopeless?

God did not arrange a perfect world for Jesus to live in, but He did provide a way for Him to accomplish His mission. That sounds exactly like the plan God has for you and me! We don't live in a perfect world either, but God has made provision for us to accomplish the mission He has for us.

I eventually came to understand that Jesus gives us the power to live in this world without being controlled by it. Jesus wants it to be simple, not complicated. He taught us to become more like little children – able to believe.

When Thomas was finally able to see and touch Jesus, he was excited! It was then that he believed Jesus had been resurrected from the dead. But Jesus told him it would have been better if he could have believed *without seeing*. We can believe that Jesus is with us even when we see little evidence that He is.

Evidence comes as a result of our faith.

Each day I'm learning that I don't have to see Christ with my own eyes or hear Him with my own ears in order to experience His joy. Such evidence is a natural result of taking the simple steps of faith to believe that:

*All that happens to us is working for our good if we love God and are fitting into His plans.* (Rom. 8:28)

Jesus loved His Father and is now seated at God's right hand, forever. The apostles suffered much, but they will be honored throughout eternity as the men who caused Christ's Good News to spread around the world.

Now it is our turn. We, too, will experience problems and suffering. But we can also receive many good things. God wants us to understand:

*... how incredibly great His power is to help those who believe Him. It is that same mighty power that raised Christ from the dead . . . .* (Eph.1:19)

Think of it: the same power that raised Jesus from the dead is available to help you and me! Talk about a reason to rejoice!

Just as the lame man responded when Jesus

said, *Pick up your bed and walk*, let's pick up our problems and walk! It wasn't easy for the lame man to believe he could stand up. After all, if he tried and fell flat on his face the people would laugh and jeer at him. And it isn't easy for us to believe that God can fill and fill and fill our hearts with His joy. But His supply is so abundant and so powerful that He can keep filling anyone who will believe Him.

The more frequently we refuse to be troubled about the details of this world, the closer we get to understanding how Jesus dealt with everything that happened to Him. He saw our world from God's perspective. *This gave Him power!* And He said we could have His power. One step at a time, we can move toward becoming more like Him. On our way, we can feel His joy working in us.

## Chapter 16
### *Is God Failing You?*

Walking on a lawn does not permanently injure the blades of grass. They soon spring back with buoyancy. But if we walk that same path over and over the grass will eventually wither and die. Keep treading that path and the ground begins to sink into a rut. That's the way unhappy thoughts cut a grove in our minds. Eventually we feel it would be impossible for us to be filled with joy. It's at this point that it seems as if God has failed us.

Our lack of faith is clearly demonstrated by our thoughts. If we think, "I am unhappy," that becomes a declaration of what we believe. We are saying to ourselves and perhaps to others, "God is failing me." We may not say those exact words, but we are declaring *His failure*. Such thoughts will cause a loss of the joy God designed for us.

Is God failing us? Let's take a look at what the Bible says:

*You see, at just the right time, when we were still powerless, Christ died for the ungodly.* (Rom. 5:6 NIV)

The Bible certainly agrees that we have a need, and that we are *powerless* to help ourselves. God's solution to that need? Christ's death on the cross. By His death on the cross:

*[Jesus] bought our freedom with His blood and forgave us all our sins.* (Col. 1:14)

There it is! Do you see it? Because of what Jesus did for us, we can be forgiven! God has the authority to forgive us. Let's consider this concept in more familiar terms.

The President of the United States has the authority and power to write a pardon for John Doe. The President doesn't need to list his reasons; he signs his name and the pardon is final. It doesn't matter if John has stolen one billion dollars or murdered someone.

John Doe is sitting in his prison cell when the warden of the prison receives word of the pardon. The Warden may think the pardon is absolutely wrong, but he has no say in the matter. He must release John Doe.

The Governor of the state may be angry and want to stop the pardon, but there is nothing he can do. There is no person, board or official he can appeal to, not even the Supreme Court! John Doe goes free – period!

Furthermore, the courts will not label John Doe as a convicted criminal. His record is clear – as clean as if he had never committed a crime.

Try to imagine the joy that John Doe has when he receives this good news! It is an awesome power that the President of United States has.

God's power to forgive sin is far more incredible. He has the power to forgive any sin, of any kind, no matter what it is. If John Doe asks God to forgive him – and believes that He does – God will never hold John's sins against him.

Some folks honestly feel that their past has been so bad, or their mistakes so stupid, that they don't deserve to be forgiven or to have great joy in this life. They cling to unhappiness as a sign of their true repentance. But God does not want to be treated as if He were a man. He is Almighty God. He wants us to have the joy that comes when we believe that He *completely* forgives us.

The more frequently we speak and sing about His power to forgive, the greater our confidence and joy become. We grow to be like the young son of the President of the United States. He could say to his friends, "My dad can get us an airplane or a ship anytime we want. If I do anything wrong my dad can give me a Presidential pardon."

"For anything?"

"Yes, anything."

God's forgiveness is proof that He is not failing us. He has acted, and He *is* acting, on our behalf. God's forgiveness will change our lives if we allow it to.

I saw a man being interviewed on television who was introduced as having sold more recordings than any other recording artist. At one time he had sunk into the pit of drugs and alcohol and nearly lost everything.

When asked what caused his downfall, he gave an unusual answer. He had felt guilty because he was so successful! He had thoughts in his mind that accused him of being so horrible that he deserved to be sick and die.

The man said he eventually asked for God's forgiveness, received Jesus as his Savior, and then his mind became clear. He knew that God loved and forgave him. As Scripture says, Satan is a liar and the accuser. He will accuse us of anything that can make us unhappy.

Satan hates the "injustice" of God forgiving people just because they ask Him to do so. Satan may tell John Doe over and over, "You're only kidding yourself if you think your crime is wiped out just because the President pardoned you." If John didn't know better, he could live the rest of his life feeling afraid that the police might take him back to prison to finish his life sentence. In the same way, Satan might say to us, "When you die you will suffer – wait and see."

We may waver in believing that God really forgives us, but when God signs a pardon for sins, the pardon is final and complete. He wants our *trust* and *joy* to be complete.

Why would Satan be concerned about our having joy in being forgiven? It's because of the change that might happen in us when we realize the enormity of the gift we have received. Forever forgiven! We might be so happy that we praise God with excitement and others will notice and want to be forgiven also.

Our enemy is not worried about what *we* want, but what *God* wants. So Satan presents us with thoughts that he thinks might prevent us from falling head over heels in love with God.

Satan is always striving to find ways to make us unhappy and to keep us from the joy God wants us to have. We need to be aware of his schemes so we can resist him. One of the ways he tries to make us unhappy is by tempting us.

Satan tempted Eve through food and he tempted Adam through a woman. Since then, Satan has studied every person to determine how to successfully tempt them. He watches our responses to everything and waits for the most opportune moment to unleash his chosen plan. Study the lives of people in the Bible and you'll see how successful Satan has been.

Each person is completely different. There are twelve billion eyes, sixty billion fingerprints, trillions of strands of DNA, and all are different. Beside all these differences, each person has experiences that make him or her unique, unlike any person who has ever lived. No person will ever think, feel and react exactly as you do! You are unique, and your temptations are uniquely planned.

How often do we complain that God is failing us, when in truth, we are unhappy because we've fallen into temptation?

We also tend to think that God is failing us when we are fearful. Fear has its place, but can be used against us when it is out of place.

To begin our relationship with God, we must reverently fear Him – bow in submission and ask for His forgiveness. Sometimes people continue in that same relationship with Him and never get any farther. God wants us to go beyond fear – way beyond. He wants us to receive His forgiveness and go on to know who He is, and what He wants to do for us. He wants to teach us the incomparable greatness of His forgiveness. We are to fear God, but also have great confidence in what He has done for us.

On the other hand, Satan wants us to dwell on our past sins, the probability that we will commit more, and the fear of facing God. When we dwell on these things, God seems distant. More than that, it seems as if He has failed us. It's true that the Old Testament says much about fearing God, but the New Testament declares that:

*All these new things are from God who brought us back to Himself through what Christ Jesus did. And God has given us the privilege of urging everyone to come into His favor and be reconciled to Him.* (2 Cor. 5:18)

Our faith in Jesus helps us to fellowship with God, but fear can prevent the closeness that God wants us to enjoy with Him.

Fear is like water in our gasoline tank. Water has its place, but if it gets into the gas tank of a car, it defeats the power of gasoline. Fear also has its place, but it can prevent fellowship with God. We must have fellowship with God in order to experience His joy and be an example of His *secret weapon*. We sometimes think that by being fearful we are only being humble, but we can't be humble enough to get anywhere near God! It is only *through Christ* that we have the honor of approaching the Father.

Fear is a physical reality and it carries with it an odor. Consider a simple house pet: a dog can smell fear. We can't smell fear, but we do feel it.

Satan does his best to control us by fear. When Peter urged Jesus not to go back to Jerusalem where He might be killed, he was speaking in fear. Jesus told Peter that Satan was speaking through him, and Jesus wanted no part of being afraid.

If we are afraid of God, our joy will never be any greater than it is right now. But when we rejoice in what God has done for us, our joy will *soar on wings like eagles.* (Is. 40:31)

How about when we suffer? Do we think God is failing us then? God has the power to end all suffering. But He is interested in more than making us comfortable. He wants us to grow in Christ and learn to use the power He has given us. Even Jesus learned from His suffering:

*Although He was a Son, He learned (active, special) obedience through what He suffered . . . .* (Heb. 5:8 AMP)

Suffering can do more than just make us feel its presence. It can control our joy. It easily becomes the center of our universe, and it will, unless we learn that that is God's rightful place. God does not give us the power to end all suffering, but He gives us the freedom to decide how we *react* to suffering.

Doctors have only limited power over our pain. Painkillers eventually wear off and the body can develop an immunity toward them. Pain seems to rule, and it has appeared to be that way all our lives. Over time, pain and suffering can grow "roots" into our bodies and minds. We think, "If God loved me He would take away my suffering." Sometimes we go so far as to say, "*If* God takes away my suffering, *then* I will know that He loves me. And if He does, I promise to tell everyone what He has done." When He doesn't respond to our accusations or bargaining we can become bitter – even doubtful that He exists.

There will come a day when there will be no more suffering, but that day is not yet here. In the meantime, God has revealed a "secret weapon" to control the *effect* suffering has over us.

I don't enjoy physical pain. And I'm not always able to turn the pain off just because I would like to. If we can't turn it off, how can we possibly have power over pain?

Jesus' disciples learned amazing things about suffering. They learned to rejoice even when they had to endure *unusual pain*. That does not sound natural, but it was the key to their experiencing such *unusual joy.*

The disciples rejoiced after being beaten because God had *counted them worthy to suffer* for believing in Jesus (see Acts 5:41). James said:

> *Consider it pure joy, my brothers, whenever you face trials of many kinds . . . .* (James 1:2 NIV)

Yes, the disciples suffered, but they realized that the power of God was working in them in ways that they had never before understood. When we rejoice over suffering, it no longer controls our thoughts. Instead of feeling put down, stomped on and defeated, we will feel ourselves surrounded by God's love. Rather than feeling abandoned by God, we feel empowered by Him!

With their attitude toward suffering, the disciples were set free from the fear of telling others the Good News. They knew there was a chance they would be arrested, beaten, or even killed. Yet they fearlessly gave Christ's message to people who heard and believed. Do you see how powerfully God's "secret weapon" worked, and is still working?

We are tempted to become discouraged when we suffer, but as we come to see suffering as God sees it, we become certain that it will work for our good.

There are spiritual forces that despise God's plan. They are continually at work to try to make us unhappy. Satan gives us *many* unhappy thoughts that we can accept or reject. One powerful way to refute them is to have in the front our mind, "God is working for my good." That is the promise He gives us in Romans 8:28.

So why not make the decision now? "No matter what happens, I believe God will make it work for my good!" Fortify that attitude over and over until it becomes a major part of who you are.

When we look at the world around us, we see pain and suffering and a great deal of evil. But God has not failed us. He has a plan for our broken, desperately wicked world.

He was willing to make the ultimate sacrifice: He gave us His Son. He even offers to share *His joy* with us!  He who created our entire universe shared His best with us. He could have backed up time, wiped out everything He created, and even declared that we never existed! Mankind would be gone.

Instead, God decided to make a big change in anyone who would accept His gift of forgiveness. He declares all those who believe as "not guilty" – of sin, faults and failures. Then He added another amazing gift: the gift of His joy!

145

An old friend of mine, Warren Anderson, used to say, "What a deal." God's joy is designed to fill us to overflowing when we receive what He has done for us out of His goodness. Of course, if we don't realize His love and goodness toward us, we are likely to feel and act unhappy. What a waste that would be!

Electricity has been available since the beginning of creation, but men had to learn how to use it. Our Father promises to give us joy, here and now, if we will believe Him. But His power is useless to us unless we learn to use it. In Heaven we may say, "How ignorant I was for being an unhappy Christian! Why didn't I learn to receive the joy that God made available to me?"

God will give us any amount of joy that we are willing to receive. What an offer! But people find it difficult to receive God's gift because it is a gift we must *keep on* receiving – just as we must *keep on* breathing in order to live. He challenges us to believe that all of His power is available to work for our good. His power plus our faith equals His joy in us! And His joy never fails.

This world will fail you. People will fail you. You may even fail yourself. But God has not failed you, and He never will.

## Chapter 17
### *Joy In Tragedy*

Our world is indeed a broken world. It is by no means a happy place. Yet, God tells us to be joyful *always* (see 1 Thes. 5:16).

People sometimes ask me how they can possibly praise God when they have lost that which was the center of their happy life. They are hurting and they need answers. The perfect answer is found in God's wonderful promise to make *everything* work for our good if we believe Him.

What we *believe* can give us joy even when the most severe difficulties are thrust upon us. I've seen Christians fall apart when tragedy strikes. I've also seen Christians become stronger in their faith when terrible afflictions come.

The disciples truly loved Jesus and they wanted Him to stay with them. But Jesus told them it was necessary that He leave them. This seemed like a tragedy to the disciples, but today we understand why it was necessary! This is such a good example of how God takes tragedies and works good for us out of them. He wants to do the same with the tragedies that come to you and me.

How do we find joy when we have just suffered a tragedy?  There is an extraordinary answer in the Bible, describing a special blessing that God has made available to us:

*They that wait upon the* LORD *shall renew their strength . . . they shall run and not be weary . . . .* (Is. 40:31)

We seniors get very tired when we run. How can we possibly not be weary? By understanding what "weary" means.

Young people run and get tired, but not *weary*! They expect to run again in a matter of minutes. Older folks may expect to run again in a year or two – or maybe never.

Those who do not know how to receive joy become more than just *tired* when they experience a tragedy; they become weary. They endure the tragedy for months, even years. Each day they can become increasingly weary.

Those who learn how to receive joy as a gift from God expect to recover rapidly. Why? Because they know that God works everything out for their good. Recovering is part of having faith. I've seen this principle working in my own life, and in the lives of other people. God has provided His joy to help us recover from heartbreaks!

Our eyes bring us joy when we see something pleasing, and with our ears we enjoy pleasant sounds. But these things can fail: scenery changes, sounds fade, and we can lose our eyesight and hearing. We have many sensations that please us, but this book isn't about any of these. God's Word tells us about a joy that can fill our hearts. This joy never fails. It lasts when temporary pleasures fade away.

We generally derive joy from what we love. Love, like fear, can be displaced. We will not experience the fullness of God's joy if we love something or someone more than we love Him. The Bible reveals truths that are sometimes difficult – but important – for us to grasp:

*Do not love the world or anything in the world.* (1 John 2:15 NIV)

Many people have nothing but temporary happiness, and they are devastated when that happiness is taken from them.

When someone we love dies, life can become intolerable if all our happiness resided in that person – be it our spouse, child, parent or friend. God wants us to have an inner happiness that depends on *Him* – not on people or things.

If we love something, it is difficult to be happy when we are deprived of it. Sometimes we have to endure the loss of "things of this world" in order to understand that we have been depending on them for our happiness.

I've always enjoyed dogs and have learned many things while training them. They love food, and especially a good, juicy bone. Have you ever tried to take a bone from a large, untrained, hungry dog? Dogs cling to – and fight for – anything that pleases them or satisfies their hunger. In the same way, you and I may cling to and desire the things that give us pleasure.

What is the best way to take a bone from a dog?

Give him a steak!

Jesus came to give us something that is far better than the "bones" we cling to. He wants to divert our attention from the temporary happiness of this world to the eternal joys He knows God has planned for us. And He knows that once we center our attention on God's will, we will no longer be like a dog that clings to a bone.

We can learn to have more of Christ's fullness, and then learn how to share that life with others who are unhappy and "hungry."

Life isn't easy. Difficulties, stress, and yes, tragedies, do come. But what if God has made a joy available that does not depend on other people or other things? What if He wants to give us happiness that is even greater than anything we have ever experienced? What if I were to tell you that this is, in fact, the case?

**God's joy is powerful**. It is powerful because it is *God's secret weapon*.

God's supernatural joy does not come as a result of happy music or an exciting sermon, or something marvelous that another person does for us. His "secret joy" comes only through faith in the promises Jesus gave us.

I experienced God's secret joy for the first time when I was able to believe that He was filling me with His Holy Spirit. I laughed without knowing why as joy flowed from within me. The Holy Spirit had suddenly overwhelmed me. That uncontrollable joy lasted for several hours. I was forty-two years old, and no one had ever told me that such overwhelming joy was available.

My second experience with uncontrollable joy came when God introduced me to His Spirit of Praise. Nothing in this world motivated that experience. The Spirit simply overwhelmed my feelings and emotions once again with a joy that lasted for about thirty minutes.

Since that day, over forty years ago, I have been learning how I, and all God's children, can receive His joy.

I've known the power of joy working in my life,

and I've seen it working in the lives of other people, but I'm increasingly aware of just how powerful it is! God uses it to accomplish His highest purposes. He wants all people to come to know Jesus as their Savior (see Rom. 1:16 and 2 Peter 3:9). The joy that we have access to as God's children draws unbelievers to Him like nothing else can!

## Chapter 18
## *What Is Real?*

*The heart is the most deceitful thing there is, and desperately wicked. No one can really know how bad it is!* (Jer. 17:9)

What a negative thing to say. Why would anyone be so pessimistic about we who were created in God's image? Yes, there are some bad people, but aren't there more good folks than bad ones?

We just read our answer. There we have it: God's words as recorded in Jeremiah 17:9. Our hearts are "most deceitful" and "desperately wicked."

And yet we try to convince other people that we are not what we are. That's not even the worst of it. We, ourselves, become convinced that we are what we are not. We become mixed-up people in a mixed-up world.

Each of us *is* what we *are*, but nothing in this world is what it *seems to be*!

Ptolemy thought the earth was at the center of the universe. Now we know that our earth is a small planet amongst trillions of bodies, millions of times larger than our tiny earth.

At one time men decided to count the number

of stars. They estimated that there are 2,000 of them. Astronomers now believe there are eleven trillion stars to *every one person* on earth! That would be eleven trillion times six billion. That's a lot of stars! Surely the Creator of all that can do anything He wants.

Our Father created a universe so huge that we cannot even imagine how far it reaches. Yet, He gave *Himself* as a sacrifice so that we might overflow with joy! He decided to make us His adopted children! Is it possible to think of that and still say that there is nothing that gives us great joy?

God offers to recreate us. We can be "born again," forgiven of all our deceitfulness and wickedness. Christ is the architect of this new creation. God wants us to see ourselves as *His new creation*, and to be so pleased with this newness of life that we are filled with joy – great joy!

*When someone becomes a Christian he becomes a brand new person inside. He is not the same any more. A new life has begun!* (2 Cor. 5:17)

We can choose to see ourselves as a brand new people, or we can choose, instead, to see ourselves as the same old people we once were. If we do that, we will see little reason to have great joy.

I am reminded of a story I heard many years ago.

A pastor went to see one of the men who attended his church; he found the man plowing a field with his team of horses.

"John, I've come to ask you for a favor. People in the church have asked me to talk to you about the way you behave in church. You get so excited that you start shouting. They say you distract them from worshiping the Lord."

The man said, " Oh Pastor, please forgive me. I don't mean to disturb anyone. It's just that sometimes I get to thinking of how bad I used to be and all the terrible things I used to do. Then I remember how wonderful I felt when I asked God to forgive me. Oh, how happy I got! Oh, pastor please hold these reigns for me for a spell, I've just got to shout for a while!" And he ran across the field shouting, "Praise the Lord! Praise the Lord!"

We need a joy so powerful that it overcomes any natural reluctance to realize that God has created a new person in each of us!

God used the New Testament to record the way He wants us to see ourselves: forgiven; adopted as His children; destined for Heaven. He says *Christ's righteousness* is now *our righteousness* (see 2 Cor. 5:21). We may think, "I don't see myself that way." But remember, we don't see *anything* as it is. We see a steel bar, but cannot conceive of it being composed of trillions of atoms. We look up at the stars, but can't imagine that they make up less than one-trillionth of one percent of the universe!

God wants us to grasp the enormity of His gifts to us.

If you were to think of yourself as nobody and nothing, you would be deceived! If you have asked God to forgive you and have received Christ as your Savior, you are no longer the desperately wicked and deceitful creature you once were. You are a child of God! The more we understand how *God* sees us, the greater our joy becomes. It is for this reason we can look at everything around us and think, "I'm not what I seem to be, either. I am destined for Heaven's glory."

God made you, with all your flaws, to show His almighty power. He sees you as you really are – His beloved child. For our own benefit, we need to learn how to see ourselves as God sees us. Remember, He sees us *through His eyes*!

The way we think about ourselves is so very important. We habitually think that we are unworthy of love or of God's blessing. Of course we *were* unworthy. But we are not the same anymore. A new life has begun. We learn to believe whatever our thoughts keep repeating. So read what God has to say about you, and keep telling yourself these truths:

*You are no longer a slave, but a son; and since you are a son, God has made you also an heir.* (Gal. 4:7 NIV)

You may not *feel* like a child of God, but that is what the Bible says you are if you have put your faith in Christ. So we must ask ourselves, "What is real?" The *truth* is what's real. We can't depend on what we see in this world because nothing is what it seems. For example, the Bible says that death is not the ultimate end:

*Whoever lives and believes in Me will **never die.*** (John 11:26 NIV, emphasis added)

When our bodies die, we are instantly alive with Christ!

Seconds before my father died, he sat up in bed and said, "Look! They are here to meet me." He died before he could explain who "they" were. I've always thought that it was the angels who were sent to usher him to his new home. Before my Grandmother Carothers died she said to me, "I hear the music. Don't miss it. Merlin, don't miss it!" Before my brother David Bert died, he pointed and said, "Look, Jesus is here!"

I am pointing your attention to Jesus and saying, "He is alive! He lives to give you great joy!" He wants you to believe that because of Him you have a new life that is overflowing with great joy!

Chapter 19

# *Power Pushing Us Upward*

We have the wonderful potential to receive joy that enables us to draw another person to Christ. Joy in the Christian can be to the unbeliever what sweet nectar in a flower is to the honeybee. But beware: our enemy is seeking for ways to push us downward.

As an Army chaplain, I often listened to men's day-after reports following their efforts to experience sexual pleasure. Perhaps the men only gave me their negative reports, but they were many. Their expectations of enjoying an evening of ecstasy had always been shattered. They felt cheated. Yet, there would be a next time: they would try again, still hoping to find satisfaction – only to be disappointed once again.

As if this weren't bad enough, some men experienced far worse results: they acquired a disease that would stay with them for life. The devil's motto is, "Have fun now; worry about the cost later."

God's passion for His children is that we have joy today and even greater joy in the days to come. He wants us to learn how we can have joy even when Satan is using his most unfair tactics against us. You and I can receive a portion of the passion that God has! We can convince others that God's joy is real.

I receive many letters from people who report wonderful benefits from reading what I have written about the importance of having a joyful heart. These readers often want to help other people.

Some time ago, the Office of the Chief of Navy Chaplains called me to order some books. They made the unprecedented decision to obtain 900 copies of *Prison to Praise* and to give one to every chaplain in the U.S. Navy. With each book, they included a letter encouraging the chaplains to obtain copies that they could give to their people.

Then the Office of the Chief of Army Chaplains requested copies for every Army Chaplain, and they, too, encouraged each chaplain to contact us. Many military chaplains have now requested free copies for their people.

The producer of a television network purchased 100,000 copies of *Prison to Praise* to send to people who contacted them. He also wanted to help people.

Early Christians sang as they waited for hungry lions to attack them. Did they actually have joy? They had enough joy to convince some of the unbelieving Roman spectators that Christians had something they needed. Out of these horrible persecutions sprang a revival that spread all over the world! Many came to believe that what Jesus had taught was true:

*I say these things while I am still in the world, so that My joy may be made full and complete and perfect in them that they may experience My delight fulfilled in them, that My enjoyment may be perfected in their own souls, that they may have My gladness within them, filling their hearts.* (John 17:13 AMP)

When I read these words that Jesus gave us, I am filled with His delight! You and I can be witnesses that what He said was true! We can say to hurting people, "God has a secret He wants to share with you!"

For 2,000 years unhappy people have discounted spiritual joy as unobtainable for "normal" people like themselves. But Jesus revealed that God wants to share His gifts with the weakest, most sinful individuals on earth.

I'm learning that I can have joy, regardless of my own failures, so long as I follow one rule: I must believe Jesus NOW. Not at some future time, but *now*. It is *now* that I am receiving His free gift of great joy. This gift gives me the energy that I need to *rejoice in the Lord always.*

Satan is always trying to pull us down, just as he tried to pull down Jesus and His disciples. But one day the battle will be over. All the forces of evil will be defeated. There will be nothing for us to fight against!

For now, God calls us to be a light on a hill that shows others the way to the One who came to bring "joy to the world."

Why doesn't God make life easy for us, so that Christians might be involuntarily filled with happiness? A seed takes months, or even years, to produce its fruit. That's the way God designed it. And He designed you and me so that we will enjoy His gifts *when* we *believe Him*!

Do Christians have more joy than non-Christians? The answer should be yes, but you probably know that's not always the case. How can this be true when God has promised to give us great joy?

God told the Israelites that the Promised Land was theirs. But they didn't believe He would help them to possess it. Therefore, for many years they lived unhappily in the desert.

*They were not able to enter, because of their unbelief.* (Heb. 3:19 NIV)

We live in our own "desert" of unhappiness

when we fail to believe God and claim the joy that Jesus promises us. The Promised Land was symbolic of what God was planning to give all His children through Christ. We can possess His promises through faith!

Every day there are many opportunities for us to choose either unhappiness or joy. Every situation begs a choice. For example: the driver in the car behind you honks his horn. Your natural reaction is not joy. But you have a choice: you can become irritated, or you can choose to believe that God is allowing that driver to test you. Perhaps the driver shouts at you. He isn't shouting blessings, but you can still rejoice because you know that God loves you and cares for you. The choice is yours.

Many of our choices must be made in an instant. In that moment of decision we draw on all our past experiences and the thoughts stored in our memories. What have you stored in your mind? The following are a few of the things I will not think about if I want to have joy, because God has foreordained them to *decrease* my health and joy: anger; resentment; hatred; worry. Life is too short to waste any time thinking on these things.

*[Life is] a mist that appears for a little while and then vanishes.* (James 4:14)

Time is too precious for us to waste. You may think that you have so many reasons to be unhappy that it is too difficult to ignore all of them. Try believing that somehow God will use at least *one* of your problems to accomplish something good. Each time you turn a thought of unhappiness into one of joy, it will be easier to transform another one.

I well remember some of the things that once devastated my peace of mind. Gradually, my attitude toward these things changed. With each victory I found myself better prepared to face greater and more difficult challenges.

So, start where you can. Be victorious when you can. Keep moving forward.

Remember that our challenge is to rejoice in the Lord ALWAYS. Don't put off rejoicing until your situation changes. God may be – and probably is – waiting for *you* to change. We often want this, that or the other thing to change *before* we truly believe that God will supply whatever we need. But that's not the way it works. God wants us to believe *first*.

In the seventeenth chapter of John, Jesus told the Father that He had finished His work. Jesus has done His part, and now we have the opportunity to do our part: believing God. Jesus knew that His disciples, as well as future believers, would face all kinds of troubles. But with believing comes an ever-increasing joy in what God is doing in us! We will never be victorious if we wait for our situation to change.

After years of being chained in prison, Paul said this:

*I have **learned** to be content whatever the circumstances.* (Phil. 4:11 NIV, emphasis mine)

Most of us have not matured to the level of being content *whatever the circumstances.* But Paul didn't tell us this so we would feel guilty when we are discontented. He wanted us to know that we can *learn* to have this same contentment that he had. His happiness did not depend on his circumstances. How could that be? He believed that God was in charge of his life. He knew that when God wanted him out of prison, He would take him out!

We do not have to suffer the intense pain and difficulties that Paul did as he learned contentment, but if we can learn how to be content in even *one* difficult circumstance, we will better understand the secret of living in joy. The reality is that God is looking for people He can bless!

When God wants our situation to be changed, He will change it. When He wants *us* to do something, He will help us do it. Believing this gives us a spirit of contentment, even joy.

165

Picture a cut flower that is limp and sagging downward. Place that flower in a vase filled with water, and soon a marvelous thing happens: the flower revives and lifts upward!

What power is in the water that could possibly push a flower upward? Flowers are composed mainly of water. When fresh cut, flowers are filled with water and that holds them upright. When placed in an empty vase, flowers begin to wilt because they are cut off from their water supply. They must have water if they are to flourish. Now if you were to add water to that empty vase, you wouldn't see the water doing anything – even if you watched the process carefully. All you would see are the results. The same is true of faith. We cannot *see* faith, but it brings new life into our bodies. Faith "pushes us upward." When you believe God's promises, that belief brings a smile to your face, changes the way you speak, puts new purpose in your step, and may even add an inch to your height!

When God gives us a smile, it resides in our hearts and has remarkable power to influence every part of our lives. Even the spirit-world takes notice when a happy person comes on the scene. Angels are blessed and evil spirits cringe when they see God's presence in a happy heart.

God designed the flower so that it is changed when it works *with* water. He designed us so that when we work *with* what He teaches in the Bible, we are also changed! When we are "sagging downward," His joy lifts us upward.

Believe that God *is* working in you. He moves in us when we *believe* Him. Some people feel a change taking place in them the moment they believe that Jesus is their Savior, and others feel that change later. It is important that we not feel discouraged just because God doesn't work in us the same way that He does in another person. And we must not discount another person's experience simply because theirs is not like our own. Each of God's children is His unique creation.

As you believe that God is doing something good in and for you, picture water flowing up into a flower, bringing it strength and beauty. Continue to practice believing, and you will eventually see God's promises being fulfilled in you.

Remember, a flower can't push itself upward – the water does that. Consider the person who says, "I've been too unfaithful for God to answer my prayers." Our enemy always tries to stress our weakness, but God wants to emphasize the strength of His Son and what *He can do in us*! God designed the flower to draw water upward, and He designed us to draw strength and joy from our faith in Jesus.

Joy gives us the strength to stand, and we can

only draw that joy from God. He is our source. After all, joy is *God's **secret weapon***. He uses it to build us up and to attract others. Share your joy with everyone you meet: it shouldn't be a secret!

## THE END

## *Postlude*

Mary and I have read every page in this book many times. Each reading has increased our own joy. We encourage you to re-read each page.

If this book has been a blessing to you, please let us know. Every month we prepare *Praise News* in which we share new things that we learn about praise. We will be pleased to send this to you at no charge, on request. You can contact us at:

Foundation of Praise
PO Box 2518, Dept. B21
Escondido, CA 92033-2518

Or visit us at www.merlincarothers.com

172

## You will also want to read these other best-sellers by Merlin R. Carothers

**Prison to Praise**.......................................................... **$4**
Many people list as the most unusual book they have ever read. Millions say it changed their lives and introduced them to the solution to their problems. This is not a book about a prison with bars, but about a prison of circumstances–and how to be set free!

**Prison to Praise, read on CD** ................................... **$14**

**Prison to Praise, Video**............................................. **$10**

**Prison to Praise, DVD**............................................... **$16**

**Power in Praise** ......................................................... **$9**
Learn how the principles introduced in *Prison to Praise* work in every day life.

**Power in Praise, Read on CD** ................................ **$15**

**Answers to Praise** ..................................................... **$7**
Overjoyed Christians felt compelled to share with Merlin the "signs and wonders" they experienced while practicing the teachings in his first two books.

**Praise Works!** ........................................................... **$7**
More letters from an assortment of thousands illustrate the secret of *freedom through praise.*

**Walking and Leaping** ............................................... **$9**
When Merlin and his family rolled over a hill in their new car and trailer they praised the Lord and miracles happened!

**Bringing Heaven into Hell**........................................ **$9**
Merlin shares new discoveries of how the Holy Spirit sheds light from heaven in the midst of a personal hell.

**Victory on Praise Mountain** ...................................... **$9**
Spontaneous praise often leads into valleys that are direct paths to higher ground.

**The Bible on Praise**..................................................... **$3**
A beautiful front cover painting by Merlin. Features Merlin's favorite selected verses on praise from thirty-eight books of the Bible.

**More Power to You** ..................................................... **$9**
Written for people in every day places who need more power in their every day lives.

**What's on Your Mind**................................................. **$9**
Would you be ashamed for everyone you know to see your thoughts? If so, you urgently need to read and understand What's on Your Mind?.

**Let Me Entertain You**.............................................. **$7**
After years of serving the Lord Merlin was eager to retire. He wanted to rest, relax and enjoy a quiet life, but God had other plans for him.

**From Fear to Faith** ................................................. **$9**
God wants to be intimately involved in your life and help you have victory over your problems.

**Praise Classics** ....................................................... **$10**
Prison to Praise and Power in Praise in a hardcover edition.

**You Can Be Happy Now** .......................................... **$9**
Everyone desires to be happy! This book will help you to understand how much God wants you to be happy.

**Secret Sins**.................................................................. **$9**
As you read this book you will be especially pleased to learn that God has provided a simple way for many of us to be delivered from our secret sins.

# AWARD WINNING MOVIE

A First Place award
by "National Religious
Broadcasters."

An Angel Award by
"Excellence in Media."

A First Place Covenant
Award by "The Southern
Baptist Radio and
Television Commission."

ISBN 987-0-943026-39-3

If you didn't believe in miracles before, you will after
watching *Prison to Praise*.

A sixty minute DVD that will be enjoyed by both
children and adults.

Available for $16.00 from:
Foundation of Praise
PO Box 2518
Escondido CA  92033-2518

## About the Author

Merlin R. Carothers' books have been translated into 58 languages. A Master Parachutist and Demolition Expert in the 82nd Airborne Division during three major campaigns of World War II. At the conclusion he served as a guard to Gen. Dwight D. Eisenhower. Later, as a Lt. Colonel in the U.S. Army Chaplaincy he served in Europe, Korea, the Dominican Republic, Panama and Vietnam. He is a pilot, lecturer and retired pastor. He has made many appearances on national television and has traveled worldwide to share what he has learned about praise.

Merlin and his wife, Mary, live in San Marcos, California.

# NOTES